I0485952

Motor Insurance Simplified

Mohammed Sadullah Khan

ISBN-13: 978-1517067908

ISBN-10: 1517067901

DEDICATION

Dedicated to my parents and family members.

Motor Insurance Simplified

CONTENTS

MOTOR INSURANCE SIMPLIFIED

ACKNOWLEDGMENTS

I would like to thank the members of my family for coping with me during my writings.

1. Introduction

The growing population has led to a growing demand for different kinds of vehicles for transporting people and the property. The high number of vehicles on the road has also lead to an increasing number of accidents due to usage of motor vehicles. These accidents have led to the death and disability of many people along with the destruction of property worth billions of dollars throughout the world. In real monetary terms it has led to huge financial losses not only to the individuals but also to the corporates, society and to the country overall. To overcome the financial losses motor insurance has played a major role in compensating the insured as well as the victims of the accidents.

Motor Insurance is also known by different names such as auto insurance, vehicle insurance, automobile insurance motor vehicle insurance and car insurance. The words, motor and vehicle have been used interchangeably.

The intention of motor insurance is to provide coverage for financial expenses incurred due to covered perils. There are different types of motor insurance policies each policy has its own limitations and exclusions. It is one of the most interesting and fastest growing sectors in most of the countries and it also comes under top three classes of business in terms of GWP (gross working premiums) from general Insurers perspective, it also consumes a major chunk of premium as far as the buyer of the insurance (whether corporate or an individual) is considered.

Each country of the world may have its own unique features and depending upon those features the requirements of motor insurances are addressed. The first policy introduced in United Kingdom with a purpose to cover the third party losses. Later on this was expanded to cover loss occurring to the vehicle it selves due to covered perils and it helped in providing different types of comprehensive coverage's.

A vast majority of countries have mandatory motor insurance. The mandatory insurance covers the liabilities to third party arising out of vehicular accident. Mandatory insurance will allow the locally registered companies to offer the products as mandated by the Governments. In case of mandatory insurance the insurance companies will be required to provide with the basic minimum coverage as mandated by the government. The insurance companies can compete in terms of pricing and quality of services. They also have an opportunity to offer better products, than the mandated products to the customers. The varieties of products offered are usually the improved versions of the mandated products.

Motor insurance is offered by the private sector insurance companies, but in some countries it is also offered by the companies owned by the governments. Hence the availability of motor insurance is from both the private sector and the public sector insurance companies. Now-a-days due to more focus on the privatization, the public sector insurance companies are being made into private sector companies or at least a substantial portion of shares are sold to the private sector or to the general public to make it more responsive to the demands and requirements of the consumers.

In most of the countries a majority of the people belong to the middle class or below middle class, hence the disposable income of these people is very low. Owning a vehicle is no more a luxury but has become a necessity. Many finance companies, banks and dealer of the vehicles offer installment schemes to promote the sale of vehicles to the customer who cannot afford a cash down payment. Due to less disposable incomes any major expense due to a vehicular accident will drain the minimal savings which an individual household is able to make.

A vehicle is treated as a dangerous animal and owning a vehicle and operating it can bring about a loss not only to the third parties but also to the insured himself. In motor insurance terminology the insured is termed as the first party and the Insurance company is termed as the second party and the rest are treated as the third parties. The loss occurring to the insured vehicle due to an accident can be estimated easily but loss occurring to the third parties cannot be easily estimated.

In some countries like USA or India the death of a third party can bring about an astronomical claim to the person responsible for the death of third party. In case of major injury the cost of damages, treatment and rehabilitation of third party can be enormous and may run into millions. It will be quite difficult for an average citizen of the country to get substantial amounts of money in a relatively short period. Many people have become bankrupt due to uninsured motor vehicle accident involving the deaths of third parties.

In view of huge costs the individuals and organizations who are engaged in the usage of vehicle should make sure that that a proper insurance is in place before driving the vehicle. In some cases due to governmental compulsion the individuals and organizations owning vehicle are required to buy insurance for their vehicles. Due to advancements in the technology and inflation, the cost of vehicles and the costs related to the claims are constantly increasing. In spite of greater awareness of motor insurance, many people do not insure their vehicles and get caught into the liabilities related to damages arising due to accidents.

One of the major purpose of mandatory insurance for the vehicles is to make sure that the victim of a vehicle accident gets financial compensation. The compensation will help the dependents of the victim to carry on with their lives. The governments work based on the statistics related to accidents and the compensation requirements of the country. This will result in working out the minimum cover to be provided by an insurer for the third party insurance coverage. Once the minimum coverage is prescribed then the insurer is left with no option but to provide the minimum required cover to their customers. The insurer also may not be allowed to choose the customers and invariably asked not to deny the coverage to the potential customers.

A vast majority of general insurance companies usually offer motor insurance. One of the major hurdle of motor insurance is that like health insurance it is considered as a attrition class of business. Hence the chances of making a loss in motor insurance is more. If the portfolio is not managed properly there are chances of erosion in the overall profit margins.

The insurance companies have to take a conscious and long term deliberate decision to service this class of business. Some insurance companies due to their competitive spirit and hunger for business have lowered their prices to procure the motor insurance business and have made heavy losses. The long fleet of businesses give a huge premium and if the loss ratio is bad then it may wipe out the insurance company itself. If motor insurance is done sensibly then it is a lucrative and challenging class of business.

Like any other insurance the benefits of motor insurance can only be availed when one is in distress, hence the servicing of customer in motor insurance is more important as the distress of the customer is too personal and difficult for an insurance company to remove it. The insurance company should be able to show empathy with the customer.

There are different types of motor insurance products available in different markets. The simplest product is motor third party insurance. If the coverage is a mandatory requirement then the coverage will be standard, there may be small variation in pricing depending upon the type of the insurance companies. The non-mandatory motor insurance as a product can be sold in isolation and sometimes it is linked to other products or classes of insurance like health insurance, motor third party insurance, personal accident insurance, and domestic insurance etc.

Due to availability of numerous insurance companies and motor insurance coverage's it becomes bit difficult to get the right cover. Even the broker will be in a dilemma to prescribe the right type of the coverage and the insurance company. Hence understanding of the motor insurance coverage and other aspects in right perspective will help in choosing the right coverage.

One of the areas plaguing the motor insurance industry is the fraud being committed by various parties involved in the insurances including agents, garages, employees of the insurers, brokers and the customers. Companies are struggling to overcome the challenges of fraud. Most of the countries have some kind of major or minor regulations related to the motor insurance industry. The regulators are doing good job in addressing the disputes, maintaining the liquidity and overall functioning of the insurance industry.

The motor insurance provides varied opportunities for both the buyers and sellers in the market. There are lots of misconceptions in the minds of the buyer in respect of motor insurance. Many insured are unaware of the location of the office of the insurers, as the covers are mostly sold by the agents either working near a road transport authority office, vehicle dealer office, super market or an independent office. They presume that the minimum third party coverage also provide coverage to the damage occurring to their vehicle, including the driver and passenger. The misconceptions have to be removed by the insurance companies in order to have a better penetration in the market. They should take the responsibility of fair and transparent way of dealing with the customers, educating them, making efforts to reach the unreachable customers and removing the major misconceptions.

2. <u>Benefits of motor insurance</u>

Motor insurance provides cover for financial losses due to accident to the motor vehicle and the liabilities arising out of the accident to the insured. The first car was made in the year 1886. The first motor policy was introduced almost a decade later. The initial cover provided was third party insurance. Subsequently the comprehensive insurance was introduced. Later on with the rapid industrialization the number of vehicles on the road increased paving the way for compulsory third party insurance. The compulsory third party insurance provided a protection to the insured against the financial liabilities involving third parties. The increasing population coupled with industrialization gave an opportunity for the auto industry to grow tremendously. The usage of vehicle for transportation of people and property helped in the development of the automobile industry. The growing automobile industry needed insurance not only as a part of mandatory requirement but also to secure finances from the banks and other financial institutions. The motor insurance has grown from the basic third party only insurance to a variety of coverage's which we will see in the later part of the book. The motor insurance provides different type of benefits to the different sectors of the economy. Let us have a look into the some of the benefits provided by the motor insurance.

1. Absorbing the cost of the major losses due to the operation of peril covered
2. Need not remain in a planning mode throughout lifetime
3. Economical cost of repairs and third party liabilities
4. Avoiding arrangement for huge money quickly
5. Getting the benefit of insurance companies network, advice and experience
6. Reducing the burden on the society and governments
7. Provision of employment
8. Motor insurance has helped in generating revenue for the government
9. Development of the economy

10. Peace of mind
11. Easing international travel

1. <u>Absorbing the cost of the major losses due to the operation of peril covered</u>

We are living in the age of unstable economic conditions with increasing inflation. In such a scenario the insured is the biggest beneficiary of the motor insurance. Many times it has been observed that due to major accident or loss and in the absence of insurance coverage many individuals have lost their entire savings made during their lifetime to pay for the losses. Many have sold their ancestral properties to pay the claims arising out of third party liabilities. This clearly puts a victim in very bad situation and sometimes he may end up taking loans, which may require a life time to settle them. An insurance policy will definitely help in avoiding bankruptcy. It helps in safeguarding the financial wellbeing of the insured their families in spite of a major vehicular accident occurring to a vehicle owned by the insured. Most of the countries have unlimited liability for death of a person due to vehicular accident. It will be difficult for an individual or even to an organization to afford such a cost and without any notice.

2. <u>Need not remain in a planning mode throughout lifetime</u>

As the accidents or loss situation can happen at any time. One need not worry throughout one's lifetime. If a yearly budget is planned, then that will take care of major expense due to eligible loss due to an insured peril. Even one event during a decade may bankrupt an individual or an organization. One need not go on saving spree to make sure that sufficient money is available for the unfortunate loss event or accident. By buying the minimum third party insurance the insured will be able to safeguard him selves against a huge potential loss. James, a 35 year old factory worker is earning US $ 2,000 per month and has an old car, camry, 2001 model valued at US $8,000. James is not worried about insuring his car as he feels that in case of an accident he will be able to afford US $8,000. But he has a minimum third party liability insurance with one of the leading Insurers. The cost of his insurance is US $ 400 per annum. If he insures for 10 years then he will be able to pay to the insurers an amount of US $ 4,000. If by misfortune he is involved in a major accident that has damaged a high value porsche car valued at US $120,000 anytime during the 10 years period. If he is fully responsible for the damage to the car then, his liability will be approximately US $ 120,000. Considering monthly wages, the claim amount is huge and unpredictable. If he buys insurance he is safe and need not worry. Availability of insurance will help him plan for the savings for the known expense rather than get a shock of unexpected claims arising due to usage of the car.

3. <u>Economical cost of repairs and third party liabilities</u>

Insurance companies with their volume of business and clout are able to obtain a good amount of discounts, which will help an individual to get the right repairs of his vehicle at a cheaper cost. The discounts are given in each and every service area provided by garages, this will make the repair of the damaged own car or third party car at an economical price. In the normal course the individuals, who visit the garages directly do not get the discount facility. If there is no insurance then the individual may end up paying anywhere between 10% - 30% over and above, what is normally charged to the insured customers. Hence buying motor insurance will help the insured in makings a savings at the time of restoring the property damaged or even defending the third party liabilities. The panel of lawyers with the insurer also will have a reasonable fee structure, which will provide a savings in the legal cost.

4. **Avoiding arrangement for huge money quickly**

Most of the vehicle accidents cause huge losses not only to the vehicle driven by the insured but also to the third party property including vehicles. There may also be death and injuries on both the sides. Thus any major accident will require a huge amount of cash for restoring the property to the pre-accident condition, settling the liabilities and treating the injured persons.

Sometimes a insured is put in a disadvantageous position due to delay in the arrangement of money required for restoring the vehicle to the pre-accident condition. If the vehicle is used for business purpose then the business will suffer. Motor insurance guarantees the payment of eligible expenses by the insurance company in a timely manner. Therefore the insured need not run from pillar to post to arrange huge amount of money suddenly. Timely restoration of the property and timely treatment of the injured will also help in avoiding a larger problems and larger costs.

5. Getting the benefit of insurance companies network, advice and experience

The insurance companies are in the business of addressing the concerns of their insured in respect of financial losses, risk management and loss prevention. They may be able to guide the insured to the right workshop and the right legal expert for repairing the vehicles and defending the liabilities arising out of vehicular accident. Many a times the risk managers belonging to the insurance companies have provided risk recommendations, which helped the fleet managers to avoid accidents and thereby save time, money and premiums. The systems and the network of garages, hospitals, doctors, lawyers and salvage disposal personnel etc. help in making it easier for the insured to deal with the accidents occurring to their insured vehicles.

6. Reducing the burden on the society and governments

Private motor insurance has helped in reducing the burden on the society and the governments. The insured by virtue of holding the private vehicle insurance is in a position to compensate the victim, who is injured or died due to vehicular accident. In the absence of insurance an individual may not have the capacity to pay the losses arising out liabilities to the third parties. During such situation the responsibility of taking care of dependents of the third parties will fall on the society or the government. This is one of the reasons for most of the governments making it mandatory for the motor vehicles to have a minimum third party liability insurance. The insurance will guarantee victims in obtaining adequate compensation for the loss or damages they suffer.

7. Provision of employment to the society

Most of the countries are experiencing a huge growth in motor insurance portfolio. The growth of motor insurance has provided opportunity of employment to automobile engineers, technicians, and related insurance professionals. The motor insurance industry has a demand for not only insurance professionals but also the engineering professionals like automobile engineers, mobile equipment experts, investigators and motor loss adjusters. They also create a demand for IT professionals and sales professionals. The generation of employment and utilization of the funds generated due to motor insurance has a great impact on the society.

8. Motor insurance has helped in generating revenue for the government

The motor insurance has generated a huge amount of money and indirectly it has created money for the government by way of taxes, stamp duties and other fees. The profits made by the motor insurance companies are taxed by the government. The employees working with the insurers are also paying their taxes to the government. The Insurers are also paying the registration fees, application fees, other deposits and licensing fees to the regulators and the government.

9. Development of the economy

The money of insured is pooled and kept with the insurance company; it is required when there is a claim settlement. Apart from the underwriting income the other source of the income for the insurers is the investment income. The insurance companies have huge capital requirements, which results in provision of huge capital to the economy. The premiums collected, deposits, reserves, unpaid claims and unearned premium and income over the years all contribute to a huge fund, which is invested in the different sectors of the economy as per regulations and at the discretion of the insurers. This investment has helped in the development of economies and contribution towards GDP.

10. Peace of mind

Motor insurance gives security and a total peace of mind to the insured against losses incurring due to covered accidental losses. It increases the confidence levels of the insured, even though he may be a very good driver. It provides satisfaction and relieves the driver from worries of liabilities. Many a times a person may be postponing or not willing to do his job, when it comes to driving the vehicle because of lack of insurance. A person having an insurance policy will have a peace of mind and becomes a good performer for self as well as for the employers.

11. Easing international travel

The world has become a global village and we see people travelling frequently from one country to another country it may be for tourism, business, pilgrimage, employment and for educational purposes etc. Most of the motor policies have jurisdiction clause of usage of the vehicle restricting the geographical location of usage to the country of domicile.   If an insured wants to travel outside the jurisdiction then he need to have an own damage extension in order to cover in an area outside the jurisdiction. However the third party liability is usually covered by the insurer's registered in the host country, hence he may have to purchase the Third party coverage at the border post or through some authorized insurer in his domicile country. A person travelling to an unfamiliar country will be

17

concerned if there is an accident during his travel. He may not be in a position to deal with it in financial terms and otherwise. This will protect the traveller from any repair costs related to the own damage portion of the vehicle and also save the host government from responsibility and the financial burden of the uninsured visitors.

Whether someone is traveling for few days or weeks, studying for a few months or years, voluntarily planning for an international motor insurance is necessary to have a productive trip abroad. Most of the countries insist upon international third party motor insurance in order to allow the vehicle into their countries. Thus International third party motor insurance helps not only in providing a pass to the vehicle but also guaranteeing international third party coverage during the period of travel. It provides ease and peace of mind during the travel period against claims arising out of third party liabilities.

3. <u>Legal aspects and principles of motor insurance</u>

In this chapter two elements are discussed the first one is the requirements of a valid contract and then the principles of Insurance both are important for the operation of an Insurance policy. Insurance policy is treated as a contract in any insurance transaction. The insurance policy is a contract between the insurance company and the insured or also known as the policy holder. The motor insurance contract is no different from other insurance contracts. The policy is subject to the law of contracts. The contract is between the insurance company and the insured. However being a complex contract it is better to have it in writing. Hence the policy is treated as the evidence of contract. The policy along with all its attachments and endorsements (amendments) is treated as complete contract. A contract to be enforceable legally should be a valid contract.

Requirements of a valid contract

A contract can be verbal contract or it can be a written contract. Insurance policy in legal terms is a contract and is subject the legal requirements of a country. Insurance being a complex area, to avoid the chances of fraud and misunderstanding a policy should be in writing. A written contract protects all the parties involved in the contract.

The proposer is the person who is interested to purchasing the Insurance from the insurance company and he proposes to the insurance company. The proposer is also known as the first party and the insurance company is known as the second party. Other than the insured and the insurer, rest are treated as the third parties.

When the proposer proposes to the insurer and the insurance company accepts, upon acceptance with the necessary consideration and fulfilling the other requirements of a contract, it becomes a contract.

Let us try to understand some basics of a contract. A contract is an agreement between two or more than two parties, which creates a legally binding relationship between them. In the court of law an insurance agreement is treated as any other contract.

There are certain minimum essential ingredients for a contract to be a valid contract, which are as follows,

a) Offer and Acceptance or Agreement
b) Consideration
c) Legal Capacity to the contract
d) Consensus
e) Legal Objective

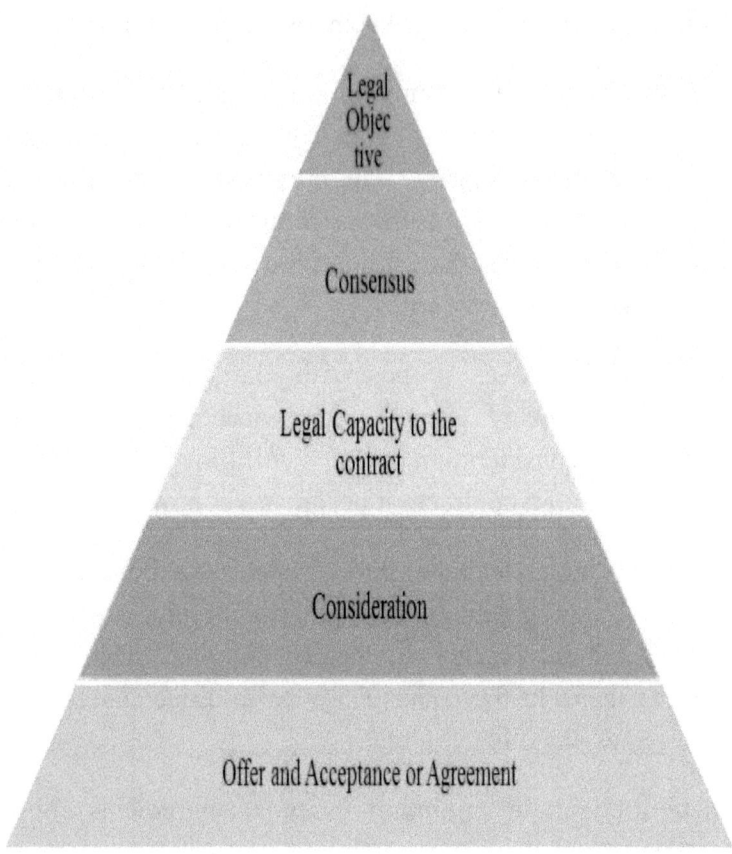

Pyramid depicting the essentials ingredients of a Contract

a) **Offer and acceptance**

The offer can be oral (verbal) or it can be in writing in the form of a proposal form. Insurance contracts being of highly technical nature it is better to have a proposal form and the policy. This will make the contract as a written contract and which is better than the verbal contract. The insured will submit the proposal to the insurance company with an intention to buy motor insurance. The Insurer will study the proposal and then if found suitable may accept or reject and in some cases will accept after certain modifications. The proposal form can go back and forth and each time it becomes an offer and counter offer. There may be few counter offers or none before reaching an agreement. Once the proposal form is accepted by the insurers then it becomes an agreement. The rules of legal contract have to be followed in order for the contract to be valid. Like the offer and acceptance should be for legitimate purpose and should be done as per the law, no coercion or fraud should be involved.

b) **Consideration**

In order for a contract to be valid there has to be a consideration. If consideration is not there then the contract will not be a valid contract. Consideration is the value offered by one party to another party. In insurance contracts the insured pays or agrees to pay the insurance premium and the insurance company promises to pay the admissible claim in case of a loss suffered by the insured. These considerations (money or services) will bind the contract.

c) **Legal capacity to contract**

One of the essential parts of contract is the legal capacity to the contract. For a contract to be a valid contract all parties to the contact should have the legal capacity to enter into a contract. The insurance company should be duly registered in the country of operation and should have the license to sell the particular class of insurance and should be capable of entering into an agreement.

With respect to juristic person, they also should be legally capable of entering into an agreement with the Insurance companies. In respect of individuals the following are not capable of entering into a legal agreement,

- Minor, a person under the legal age

- Insane person (person who is mentally incompetent)
- Being under the influence of intoxicants

d) Consensus

The parties to the agreement should have same thinking or mind. The parties to the contract of motor insurance are the insurance company and the insured. They should know the exact reason for taking the insurance policy and should be in consensus with the agreement. If the insured wants comprehensive insurance coverage and the insurance company offer him the third party liability only coverage then there is no consensus or common intention of entering into an agreement. Such agreement will not be valid as there is no consensus in the them.

e) Legal objective

The contract entered must be for a legal purpose. Insurance business is subject to regulations and most of the regulators also do the job of policing and controlling the insurance companies. However if the Insurer is not authorized to write motor insurance business and does not have a license to write motor insurance then if they are writing motor insurance policy then it becomes illegal. Similarly if the insured is insuring a vehicle, which is stolen then the legality is violated. The legal purpose is defeated in such situations and the contract will become invalid.

Special Features of Insurance contracts

Contract is an agreement which is legally binding on the parties to the contract. We have seen the legal requirements of a contract. Contract can be verbal and written. In insurance the moment there is an agreement the contract is on from the agreed date and the policy is treated as an evidence of contract. Like other business contracts insurance contracts are subject to the laws of contract. In case of breach of contract either by the insured or the insurance company the law will help in overcoming the breaches or finding the remedy to the breach. Insurance contracts have the following important features,

1. Personal Contract
2. Conditional Contract
3. Unilateral Contract
4. Adhesion Contract
5. Aleatory Contract

1. Personal Contract

In this type of contract the insurance company binds only a single insured. The insurance contract is between the insured and the insurance company and in case the insured sells his car or his property then the insurance company is not bound to cover the new insured. The coverage to the property ceases once it is sold. The new insured has to have a separate proposal and will be evaluated separately and if found suitable then the cover is provided, otherwise the insurance company based on its risk assessment has a right to refuse the cover to the new insured.

2. Conditional Contract

An agreement is considered as a conditional contract that is enforceable only if certain condition is satisfied. It is also called as hypothetical contract. The purpose of this type of contract is to make sure that certain conditions are met before the contract becomes effective. An insurance contract is a conditional contact and the insurer is obliged to fulfill its promise only upon the fulfillment of promise by the insured. If the insured does not fulfill the conditions of the contract then the insurers may not honor their promise of financial compensation.

3. Unilateral Contract

In unilateral contract only one person or group or organization to the agreement makes a promise in the agreement. Insurance contract is a typical example of unilateral contract. Insurance contract is a contract whereby the insurance company promises to pay the insured the financial compensation in case of loss occurring due to an insured peril. If the event does not occur then the Insurers are not obliged to pay anything to the insured.

4. <u>Adhesion Contract</u>

Adhesion contract is a contract wherein one party to the contract has a stronger bargaining power and is responsible for drafting the contract and the other party which is a weaker party must abide by the contract, the weaker party has very little or no power to modify the terms of contract prepared by the stronger party. The stronger party offers the contract on a take it or a leave it basis. In insurance contracts the insurance company is treated as the stronger party and the insured is considered as a weaker party. The insurance company policy is prepared by the insurers and if the insured is not comfortable with the terms and conditions of the policy he may choose to take it or leave it but usually cannot make changes to the policy document.

The adhesion contracts are lengthy and cannot be understood by layman but unfortunately it gives unfair advantage to the insurer, hence in the courts of law in case of ambiguity of wordings in the contract. The insured case is considered more sympathetically and goes against the insurer. There is nothing illegal about adhesion contract; it is used as a tool of convenience.

5. <u>Aleatory Contract</u>

Aleatory contract means that until an agreed event occurs, both parties need not perform the particular action. The meaning of aleatory is chance and the contract is dependent upon chance of occurring of an event. The amount paid by both the parties is unequal. The insured pays the premium and if nothing happens then the insured will not get anything and if there is an accident then the insurer will end up paying multiple times the premium paid by the insured. The contract is for unequal amounts depending upon a chance event.

Principles of insurance

Generally speaking Insurance in simple terms is nothing but the "losses of few shared by many". Another easy definition of the Insurance is transfer of risk (the risk is transferred from the insured to the insurance company also known as insurer). The purpose of insurance is to provide the financial protection and security to the insured from uncertainties or unforeseen events.

Motor insurance is progressing at a rapid pace as most of the governments are struggling to expedite the cases pertaining to the liability claims related to the motor accidents. Motor insurers are taking the risks of their insured, which are unpredictable and very high. However by virtue of their technical expertise they are able to contain the costs of the risks due to their effective handling of fraud, negotiations with the garages, third parties and encouragement in risk management.

The motor portfolio is termed as attrition portfolio and it requires the skills and experience of the insurance company to make the portfolio profitable. Usually most of the motor insurance policies do have different kinds of deductibles, which help the insurers in controlling the administrative and claim costs. In spite of major precautions the motor insurers have a high loss ratios hence they normally protect their losses through strict underwriting, efficient claims handling and reinsurance program. The reinsurance program helps them in reining the losses, if by chance the portfolio becomes bad.

Insurance has developed over the centuries and is a highly technical subject. The guiding light of Insurance is its six major principles. The same principles are also applied in motor insurance. In motor insurance usually insurer (who may be a composite insurer writing classes other than motor insurance or a specialist insurer writing only motor insurance) will normally takes the risk from the insured and it writes the contract and promises to indemnify the insured or his representative in case of financial losses due to an accident and or operation of a peril.

The insurance principles play an important role in the framing of the insurance contracts and claim settlement. It is also useful for the judiciary to arrive at the judgments relating to the insurance contracts. Justice cannot be done to any topic on insurance without the understanding of these principles. Understanding these principles of Insurance will help in understanding the entire subject of motor insurance in right perspective, the principles are as follows,

Understanding the Principles of Insurance

a) Utmost good faith
b) Insurable interest
c) Indemnity
d) Subrogation
e) Contribution
f) Proximate cause

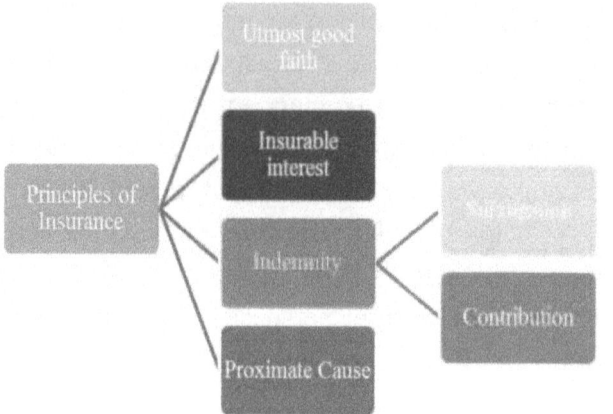

a) **Utmost good faith**

The First and the foremost principle of Insurance is the "Principle of Utmost Good Faith". In product marketing we abide by the principle of Good Faith. The product can be consumer durable goods like refrigerator, washing machine, cooker and television etc. or can be the fast moving consumer goods (FMCG) like soaps, shampoos, rice, and pulses etc. Suppose we want to buy a refrigerator we go to the showroom and buy the product by paying the price quoted by the salesman and we are not disclosing any information related to us or our activities. Even the salesman is not supposed to disclose any information unless asked for and if any information is asked by the client then he is supposed to provide the right information. It is guided by the principle known as "let the buyer beware" or in Latin it is called as "Caveat Emptor".

If you are hiring a taxi, you ask the driver to take you to a particular location and he will quote the price without him being interested in knowing anything about you. You are also not interested in getting his information and his antecedents. Once he drops you to the place agreed upon you will pay the amount agreed upon.

But insurance contracts are over and above this. They are termed as contracts of Utmost Good Faith. Utmost Good faith is nothing but it is the duty of disclosure. What needs to be disclosed is the question, which comes to our mind. We need to disclose all the information which helps the insurers in taking decision whether to insure us or to reject our proposal. If the insurer is accepting the proposal then the information helps him in providing the terms and conditions to the policy. Hence it is very essential that all the information should be provided to the Insurers.

There is a saying that right information should be provided to the doctors, lawyers and insurers. This holds good and true. Not providing the correct information may jeopardize the whole contract. In-case of doubt as to whether to provide the information to the insurer, it is better to provide the information.

Duty of utmost good faith is applicable to all the parties to the insurance contract. The insurance company should also provide the information related to its products its terms and conditions. A customer may be able to take a knowledgeable decision if he has the right information. Hence it is required on part of the insurer to provide the right and detailed information to the insured.

For individuals most of the insurance companies insist upon submission of proposal forms which contain sufficient information related to utmost good faith. Some forms also contain information as to what need to be disclosed before and during the currency period of the contract.

In motor insurance the principle of utmost good faith plays a major and important role. The increasing complexities of the motor insurance and costing of the claims and services requires that the right information is obtained from the insured. The insured on his part also should make sure that the information provided by him is factual and true to the best of his knowledge. Both the parties should have an honest and trust worthy dealings as far their contract goes. All the motor insurance contracts are the contracts of "Uberrimae Fidei", which is a Latin phrase for utmost good faith.

Duty of disclosure makes the parties to the contract to

disclose the material facts. A material fact is the fact that which influences the judgment of an underwriter or an insurer to accept or reject a particular risk and if accepted then to provide the right terms and conditions. The insured has to disclose the information and he cannot conceal the information intentionally or unintentionally. Misrepresentation or concealment of the material fact is treated as fraud. The insurance company also should disclose the facts which are relevant to the insured and may help them in taking decision like deductible, any condition which may change the understanding of the contract, policy terms and conditions etc.

Example – Mr. P is a 40 year old man and works as a cashier at one of the departmental stores. The departmental store does not provide any kind of insurance to its employees. He had an old Honda car. Two years ago and due to major accident his car was scrapped and at the time of accident he did not have any insurance. He buys a new car and one of his friends suggested him to buy a comprehensive insurance policy to cover his losses due to accidents. He goes to a local insurance company and fills the proposal form. He dutifully fills the proposal form with correct answers, however in the proposal form there was one of the questions asking him "Please give details of claims/accidents in the last five years on your vehicles, as under". He decided not to disclose his previous accident under the proposal form. He put a remark stating that "No accidents during last 5 years". This is a clear violation of principle of utmost good faith and any violation of utmost good faith will harm his claim settlement and even make the contract voidable.

Typical Question in the proposal form

Please give details of claims/accidents in the last five years on your vehicles, as under	No Accidents during the last 5 years

However there are four Facts which need not be disclosed by the insured to the insurance companies. The facts are as follows,

- Facts of law
- Facts of common knowledge
- Facts of lessening the risk
- Facts of waiver

- **Facts of law**

  Everyone is supposed to know the law of the land. The insured need not disclose if anything pertaining to the law which everyone is supposed to know. The failure of non-disclosure of facts of law will not go against the insured.

- **Facts of common knowledge**

  The Insurer is supposed to know the areas prone to accidents or other risks like floods, volcanic eruptions and if the insured does not disclose the perils in his area and insurer accepts the risk. The insured is free from blame.

- **Facts of lessening the risk**

The elements which will reduce the risk exposure need not be disclosed. Suppose the insured has installed a theft guard in his car then he need not disclose it to the insurer. The installation of theft guard will lessen the risk of theft of the vehicle. However if he has replaced his existing low powered engine with a high powered engine then he should disclose it to the insurer. The replacement of high powered engine will definitely increase the risk of accidents.

- **Facts of waiver**

The information which has been waived by the insurer cannot be used as an excuse by the insurer against the insured. Suppose for the above question "Please give details of claims/accidents in the last five years on your vehicles, as under", the insured puts a dash mark and does not provide the details and the insurance company accepts and issues the policy. In such a situation, if claim is lodged then the insurer cannot at a later date blame the insured for not providing the necessary information.

Please give details of claims/accidents in the last five years on your vehicles, as under	-

b) <u>Insurable Interest</u>

The second most important principle of Insurance is Insurable Interest. A person without insurable interest cannot buy insurance policy.

From a laymen's perspective Insurable Interest is simply ownership. A person or an entity has an insurable interest if he owns the item or subject matter to be insured. But on a broader front without ownership if a person has financial interest in a particular risk, then also it is considered as an insurable interest. The entity who is staking a claim under the policy should be the entity suffering the financial loss. This gives wider scope to the understanding of the principle of insurable interest. The garages, which are handling the vehicles belonging to the customers, can cover the vehicles of the customer in-spite of them being not the owners of the vehicle. An individual or group, who has financial interest in another person or property, can also create insurable interest. Insurable interest is also applicable to the motor insurance. For the purpose of buying motor insurance the employer may have financial interest in the vehicle owned by his employee as he has provided the loan amount to his employee. Similarly a bank or a financial institution may have interest in the vehicles belonging to an individual or an entity by virtue of providing loan on those vehicles. There are various ways of protecting the interest of the financial institution in an insurance policy, by providing single interest policy or by dual interest policy. One of the requirements of the motor insurance is that a person should have insurable interest at the time of inception of the coverage, during the currency of the coverage and at the time of claim.

Case study – Mr. S, is working as a Human Resources Manager for a company known as ABC Corporation, which due to its large group is able to insure his car at a very reasonable premium with one of the famous insurance companies. One of the friends of Mr. S is Mr. R, who wants his friend to insure his vehicle under the banner of ABC Corporation to get the benefit of premium and coverage. Individually Mr. R will not be able to get the same premium and coverage as that of Mr. S. However Mr. S is aware of the principles of insurance and he informs his friend that as ABC Corporation does not have any insurable interest in the car belonging to Mr. R, moreover he is not an employee of ABC corporation. He informs Mr. R that in case of an accident and in case of any claim, the claim will not be admissible. He suggests Mr. R to buy an individual policy at individual premium and coverage to avoid the violation of the principle of insurable interest.

c) <u>Indemnity</u>

"Indemnity" is the third most important principle of Insurance and comes into play when there is a claim. Indemnity is applied only when there is insurable interest, if there is no insurable interest then indemnity is not applicable. The principle of indemnity states that the person suffering the financial loss should be compensated equal to the loss he suffered. He should be in the same financial position after the loss as he was before the loss. The insured should neither be better off nor worse off. All contracts of motor are treated as contracts of indemnity.

Suppose an insured meets with an accident and his vehicle is damaged. The damage is to his bumper, fender and the door. Luckily the insured was not hurt in the accident. The total cost of repairing his vehicle comes to US $ 10,000. In such a scenario the insured should be paid US $ 10,000 to apply the principle of indemnity. But in practice this may not happen as policies have conditions like sum-insured, inner limits, deductible or excess and co-insurance condition etc. However the spirit of the principle of Indemnity should be followed while practicing insurance. The principle of Indemnity clearly states that the insured should neither be financially better off nor worse off from the accident or disease.

Let us take a look into following two examples where the application of indemnity is not fully complied with.

Example 1 - Application of the principle of indemnity in case of co-insurance – Mr. M, has a motor insurance policy providing comprehensive insurance coverage. His policy had a compulsory deductible of US $ 1,000.

Being a telecom engineer he was on a holiday with his family at one of the hill stations and whilst driving down the hill his vehicle skidded and hit the tree. The vehicle had a major damage like both the front lights were damaged the bumper was broken and there were damages to the radiator and battery. He took the vehicle for repairs. The total cost of his repairing the vehicle was US $ 6,000. Due to this incident Mr. M suffered a financial loss which he is supposed to be compensated. As per the principle of indemnity he should be compensated with an amount of US $ 6,000. However in this case due to deductible amount the insured is paid the cost of repairing less the deductible, which came to US $ 5,000. On the face of it the indemnity principle is not fully complied with due to the presence of deductible. Generally in practice this principle may not be applied with 100% accuracy in all types of policies but will act as a guide to the settlement of claims.

Example 2 - Application of the principle of indemnity in case of inner limit – Mr. G had purchased a full motor insurance cover, his policy also had a coverage for towing his vehicle from the site of accident to the Garage. His limit for towing extension was US$ 1,000. Once he went to a very remote and far off location on an recreational visit.

While returning he met with an accident and his vehicle was totally damaged. He arranged for towing the vehicle to his hometown. The towing company charged him US $ 1,600. When he claimed the towing bill the Insurer paid him only US $ 1,000 as per the limitation of the policy. In this case the coverage limit condition did not allow him to be fully indemnified.

The following two Principles are supporting the Principle of Indemnity.

> ➢ Subrogation

> ➢ Contribution

d) **Subrogation**

It is one of the six principles, which supports the achievement of Indemnity. Suppose any third party is responsible for the causing the damage to the vehicle or injury to the insured under the policy, then the insured has a right to claim from the party that was responsible for causing the loss due to accident to him, moreover the insured can also claim from his insurance company. This gives the benefit of two claims to the insured and he will definitely benefit from insurance. In-order to avoid such a situation, wherein the insured is in a better off position thereby violating the principle of Indemnity, the principal of subrogation is applied, which helps in the achievement of the basic principle of Indemnity.

The insurance company applies the principle of subrogation to recover cost of the damages from the third party on behalf of their Insured. In laymen terms Subrogation is nothing but assuming the legal rights of a person for which the expenses or claim has been paid. It can be termed as substitution, substituting the place of the insured.

Example - If Mr. A is driving his car on the road and Mr. B hits his car from behind as his brakes failed at the last moment. The accident had caused a major damage to Mr. A's car. The total cost of repairing the car was US $ 25,000. Mr. A has a right to recover this amount from Mr. B. But if he has a motor insurance policy then he has a right to claim from his insurer.

If the insured claims from the insurance company and Mr. B then he will be in a better position and he is benefiting out of Insurance. Hence the Insurance Company will settle the claim and will ask Mr. A to pay back the money he received from Mr. B. If Mr. B has not paid then the insurance company will ask Mr. A to provide a subrogation letter and will pursue the claim on behalf of A. Any amount recovered from B will go to the insurance company.

Subrogation is substituting or stepping into the shoes of the insured to pursue the rights of recovery from the third parties.

e) <u>Contribution</u>

This is another principle which is supporting the principle of Indemnity. In some cases there are chances that the Insured may buy more than one policy for the same risk.

This usually happens due to various reasons, like the CEO may cover cars belonging to his team as a part of his fleet under motor insurance and also the same is covered by the Administration manager under a separate motor insurance policy covering all the vehicles belong to the Company. The same car has been covered under two separate policies. Some covers overlap due to oversight and sometimes there may also be a deliberate attempt to commit fraud. If for one loss or claim, the insured approaches more than one insurance companies and each company pays for the same loss then the insured will be in a beneficial position. This situation is avoided by applying the principle of contribution, which is a supporting principle of principle of indemnity. The Insurance Companies will not fully compensate the insured against the loss but they share the loss in the proportion of their liability.

Example - If the CEO of a Company insures his sales director's car with XYZ insurance company as a part of comprehensive motor insurance policy and his administration manager includes the same car in the company motor insurance plan with ABC insurance company. This is treated as duplication of insurance and if a motor insurance claim arises on the vehicle used by the sales director. Let us assume that the cost of loss is about US $ 50,000, which is covered under both the policies. In case the insured approaches both the insurance companies and gets full settlement of the claim from both the companies, then the insured will be in a better position by obtaining a compensation of US $ 100,000 against a loss of US $50,000. This will violate the principle of indemnity.

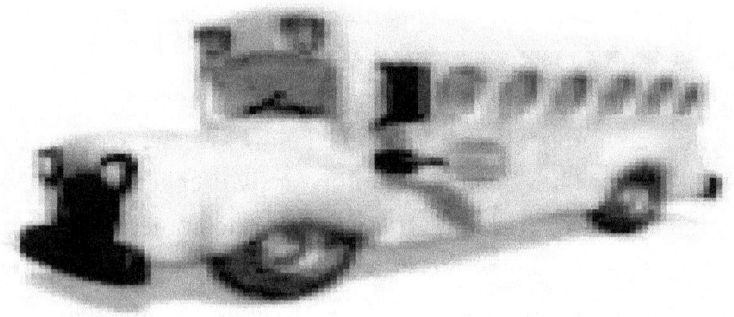

In such situation principle of contribution is applied. Assuming that the terms of both the insurance companies are similar then each company will pay the loss in proportion. Company XYZ will pay an amount of US$

25,000 and the company ABC will pay the balance which is in equal proportion. This way the Insured is not benefitted from insurance. The principle of indemnity is not violated. This way the insured will not get more than his loss. But by buying more than one policy he loses more premium, thus this principle will discourage the purchase of more than one policy by the insured and restrict the payment of claim so that the insured is not in a better position.

However if the insured buys insurance with an intention to commit fraud, then he may not get any of his claims as the contract will be treated as null and void.

f) **Proximate cause**

The last and tricky principle is known as the principle of "Proximate Cause". The purpose of this principle is to identify the peril (cause of loss), whether it is an insured peril (covered) or an excluded peril (not covered) and sometimes it may be unnamed peril. Even unnamed peril is also not covered under the insurance policy.

Normally it is difficult to pin point the cause of loss responsible for the loss or damage if there are more than one cause or overlapping causes. The Proximate cause can be the first cause or last cause or may be dominant cause. It is also defined as the cause which leads to a chain of events leading to the loss without the intervention of another event. Suppose landslide risk is excluded from the policy, whereas the flooding risk is included in the policy. If the flooding is caused by landslide, then if damage to the vehicle is caused by flooding. The risk is excluded even though the loss is caused by the flooding, which is a covered risk but the cause of flooding is landslide and landslide is not covered under the policy.

Following of the two most quoted examples will clear the purpose and application of the principle of proximate cause. A man purchases a personal accident policy (which is an accidental death cover). In the first example he is riding a horse in a cold region and he falls from the horse. His leg is severely fractured and being in a remote area, he is unable to find any help and due to severe cold he catches pneumonia and dies. In the second example the person gets help and he is shifted to a hospital and he catches pneumonia during his treatment at the hospital. After few days he dies due to Pneumonia. Here the insurance company has to decide as to which claim is payable. In both the cases there are two causes of death, accident and pneumonia, one is accidental and other one is due to a disease. The first case is treated as accidental and the claim is payable whereas the second case is treated as a death due to disease and the claim is not payable. However if the coverage is for life insurance and for death "due to any cause", then both the cases would have been covered by the Insurance Policy.

Almost all the insurance policies may have risks which are insured and some may have the risks which are excluded. To identify whether a claim is payable or not we need to know the cause of loss. Once we know the cause of loss then we will be in a position to say that a particular loss is payable or not. Proximate cause helps us in identifying the root cause of loss in case of more than one cause or overlapping causes of loss. The identification helps us to find out whether cause of loss is coming under the insured peril, excluded peril or unnamed peril.

Example – ANZ Engineering Corporation, has taken a health insurance policy, which excludes any work related accidents or diseases. One of their workers Mr. Y suffers severe back pain early morning and gets admitted to the hospital and the doctors after thorough investigations conclude that Mr. Y has an acute multiple disc prolapse. The insurance company tries to find the cause of his medical condition and they found that Mr. Y is working as a loader and un-loader at ANZ Engineering Corporation and they judge the proximate cause of the disc prolapse is related to his job function. The policy taken by the ANZ Engineering Corporation specifically excludes any loss arising out of work related diseases or accidents. The insurance company invokes this condition and denies the claim.

If the injury or disease is related to work then the claim will be admissible under the workmen compensation policy and the same should be lodged under WC policy.

4. <u>Motor insurance coverage and products</u>

Motor Insurance is currently one of the most important products in different markets. There are many types of motor insurance products available throughout the world. Understanding the basic motor insurance products will help us in understanding its variants. The basic products will give us an insight into the development process of motor insurance.

A single insurance company may have different types of products dealing with different types of vehicles. There are also many off the shelf products and these products are amended to provide new products. With the availability of technology the amendment of products has become much easier. The products may be different for corporate clients (commercial lines) and for individuals (personal lines).

In terms of coverage the motor insurance can be classified into two categories:

1) Basic third party (liability) insurance

2) Package insurance (liability + own damage cover)

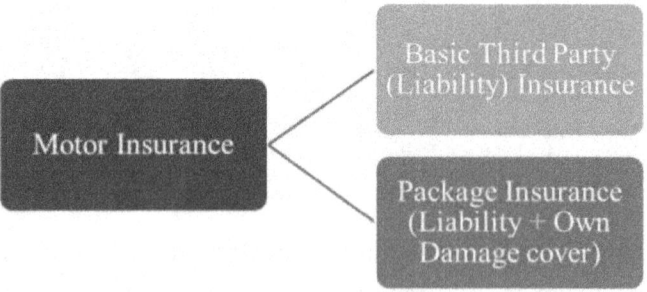

1) <u>**Basic third party (Liability) insurance policy**</u>

Basic third party (liability) insurance is the most sought after cover in the motor insurance market. In some places it is referred to as "Act" only cover, as it is a statutory requirement to have to the coverage. It can be issued as an standalone cover or can be clubbed with the own damage section of the cover. If it is clubbed with the own damage section then it is also known as package cover or comprehensive coverage. Here we will try to understand the standalone cover offered by the Insurers. In most of the countries this is a mandatory or compulsory cover. This cover is issued to different types of motor vehicles like motor cycles, commercial vehicles, private vehicles etc. There may be minor changes in the coverage depending upon the type of the vehicle. The third party covers may be branded by different names by different insurance companies but the coverage provided is similar and where the insurance is mandatory, it provides the minimum required coverage. Earlier, we have understood the concept of third party. The purpose of the cover is to provide coverage to the insured against legal liabilities against third parties arising out of the accidents, hence the coverage is popularly known as third party insurance.

Coverage

The first and important aspect of the third party cover is that it does not cover any losses occurring to the insured vehicle. The purpose is to cover only third party liabilities. The policy covers the death or bodily injury, death or bodily injury cover is also referred as simply bodily injury, caused to the third parties as a result of use of insured car. It will also provide cover to the physical damage or property damage, which means any damage caused to the property belonging to the third parties. Based on the limitation of the coverage, the third party liability (TPL) coverage's are of two major types as follows,

1) Combined limit or Combined single limit cover

2) Split limit or Separate limit cover

1) **Combined limit or Combined single limit**

Under combined single limit the coverage for property damage and the death or bodily injury are clubbed or combined together. In case of a single event the payments for the damages to the third party property, as well as payments for injury claims towards third party personal injury, would be paid out under the single limit coverage. The limit will be exhausted either in case of large single event or multiple events occurring in a year. In no case the insurance company will pay the amount beyond the agreed limit. However there are policies which will provide unlimited coverage to against liabilities arising out of accidents.

2) **Split limit or Separate limit**

A split limit or separate limit coverage policy will provide separate limits for property damage coverage and death or bodily injury coverage. In case of an accident the payments for the third party property damage liability would be paid out form the sum insured section of the property damage coverage, and payments for the bodily injuries would be paid out under the sum insured of the bodily injury coverage. Again there may be further split in the sum insured based on per person and per accident basis. In some policies the coverage under property damage may be restricted to an agreed sum assured limit, whereas the bodily injury section may have the sum assured limit or it may be unlimited.

Example

The wording of the insurance company 'A' will be as follows in case of combined single limit,

In the event of an accident occurring during the policy effective period, involving indemnity under the terms of this policy, the maximum limits of the company's liability in respect of bodily injury (including death and the sums estimated for injuries and medical expenses) and in respect of property damage shall not exceed US $ 3,000,000 (US dollars three million) per any one occurrence.

The wording of the insurance company 'B' will be as follows in case of separate limit or also known as split limit,

In the event of an accident occurring during the policy effective period, involving indemnity under the terms of this policy, the maximum limits of the company's liability per any one occurrence is as follows,

i) respect of bodily injury (including death and the sums estimated for injuries and medical expenses) shall not exceed US $1,500,000 (US dollars three million)

and

ii) in respect of property damage shall not exceed US $ 1,500,000 (US dollars three million)

The wording of the company "C" may be as follows, this is a variation under split limit covers.

In the event of an accident occurring during the policy effective period, involving indemnity under the terms of this policy, the maximum limits of the company's liability per any one occurrence is as follows,

    i)   respect of bodily injury (including death and the sums estimated for injuries and medical expenses) shall not exceed

    a) $500,000 for injury/death to one person

    b) $1,000,000 for injury/death to more than one person

    ii) in respect of property damage shall not exceed US $ 1,500,000 (US dollars three million)

2) **Package insurance (liability + own damage cover) policies**

This type of coverage was earlier known by different names such as own damage cover, comprehensive insurance, full insurance and first party insurance. But during recent times we call it as a package insurance. Here covers are added to the basic third party liability insurance. Hence the suitable word is package insurance. Depending upon different markets different covers are available to cater to the needs of the customers. Let us try to understand the different types of covers available under the package insurance as follows,

1) Collision only cover

2) Other than collision cover

3) Third Party, fire and theft insurance

4) Comprehensive specified risks insurance

5) Comprehensive all risks insurance

1) **Collision only cover policy**

Collision cover provides coverage for damage to or loss of the insured motor vehicle caused by collision peril. Usually the turning or flipping of the vehicle is also considered as collision. It will also cover collision with other vehicles and objects. However there may be confusion with many insured as well as the insurers, they may assume that collision will only cover the collision of the two moving vehicles. Which in general terminology is not correct. Some insurers clearly define the term collision to avoid the confusion in settlement of claims. Usually the coverage for collision is defined as types of covered accidents include hitting another car or hitting a stationary object, like a bridge or a tree. Collision insurance can also cover if someone or something else hits your car while it's parked.

Collision cover is usually added to the basic third party liability insurance.

2) **Other than collision policy**

Other-than-collision cover provide cover against damage from the listed perils which includes missiles or falling objects, fire, theft or larceny, explosion, earthquake, windstorm, hail, water, flood, malicious damage or vandalism, riot or civil commotion and collision with animals etc. Although collision coverage usually has a deductible, some of the perils covered under the other-than-collision coverage has no deductible. This is similar to the comprehensive cover, in this the perils are usually added to the collision cover. The coverage provided usually includes third party cover plus collision cover plus other than collision cover.

3) **Third party, fire and theft insurance policy**

This is the next level coverage after the third party insurance coverage. Most of the countries have third party liability (TPL) coverage as compulsory and hence anyone owning or using a motor vehicle need to have a compulsory TPL coverage. If someone wants to have a cover over and above this then they can get their vehicle covered against third party fire and theft coverage (TPFT). This will give them additional security, in case their vehicle is stolen or is damaged due to fire. The electronic systems in the vehicle are prone to theft and any electronic items stolen from the car also will be covered under the policy. The cause of fire may be due to many reasons, the burglar may burn the car to wipe out the evidence or a careless cigarette butt may be cause of fire or if parked in a garage then a short circuit may be the cause of fire.

This cover is usually taken if an entity owns more than one vehicle or lack of usage of one or some of the vehicles. The reason may be many like planning to sell one or more vehicles or if there is a plan to go abroad for a long vacation or simply has more than the required number of vehicles and usage is restricted to some vehicles only.

The TPFT cover is in between the TPL and comprehensive coverage it covers only two additional risks viz., fire and theft. From the insured point of view in terms of costing or premium calculation it is cheaper than the comprehensive insurance.

4) <u>Comprehensive specified risk insurance policy</u>

The coverage provided under comprehensive specified risk insurance is higher than the Third party fire and theft cover and the third party plus collision only cover. Under specified risks cover the perils covered are specified and the perils are listed in serial order, so that it is easy to identify whether a risk is covered. This can be compared to the other than collision cover, which is usually available in western countries. The comprehensive coverage also includes the coverage against third party liabilities (TPL) and also cover the fire and theft. The premium is also comparatively higher compared to other two covers discussed earlier. Due to different cultures around the world and need and requirements of the markets, similar covers may be named differently.

The wording in the specified risks policy is usually as follows,

The insurance company will indemnify the insured against loss of or damage to the motor vehicle and its accessories and spare parts whilst thereon

i) by accidental collision or overturning or collision or overturning consequent upon mechanical breakdown or consequent upon wear and tear

ii) by fire external explosion self-ignition or lightning or burglary housebreaking or theft

iii) by malicious act

iv) whilst in transit (including the processes of loading and unloading incidental to such transit) by road rail inland waterway lift or elevator

Many insurers may split the risks mentioned above or add some more risks to make it more comprehensive. But it is always short of all risks cover. Let us have a look into another offering under package insurance which is more comprehensive in nature.

a) Fire, explosion, self-ignition or lightning.

b) Burglary, housebreaking or theft.

c) Riot and strike.

d) Malicious Act.

e) Terrorist act.

f) Earthquake (fire and shock) damage.

g) Flood, Typhoon, Hurricane, Storm, Tempest, Inundation, Cyclone and Hailstorm.

h) Accidental external means.

i) Whilst in transit by road, inland waterway, lift, elevator or air.

j) By landslide/Rockslide

The above mentioned perils are named perils and the insurer will pay only if the loss of damage is caused by any of the above mentioned named perils.

5) Comprehensive all risk insurance policy

The ultimate cover under any motor policy is Comprehensive all risks insurance. The policy provides basic third party cover plus damages caused to the insured vehicle by all perils, wherein perils are not specified but exclusions are specified. Some of the insurers may have an exhaustive list of exclusions, so as to avoid the confusion in the coverage. In order to understand the all risks coverage one should know the exclusions under the policy. The usual exclusions are as under, most of these exclusions are applicable to other package covers also.

Standard exclusions:

The company shall not be liable to pay for

i)   consequential loss depreciation wear and tear mechanical or electrical breakdowns failures or breakages

ii)   damage to tires unless the motor vehicle is damaged at the same time

iii)   loss of or damage to accessories or spare parts by burglary housebreaking or theft unless the motor vehicle is stolen at the same time.

We will have a look into some of the major standard exclusions in most of the motor insurance policies.

Exhaustive exclusions under motor insurance policies

The company shall not be liable for

1. The amount stated in the policy schedule or endorsements as the deductible(s)

2. Any consequential loss or loss of use

3. Wear and tear, mechanical or electrical breakdown or failure

4. Damage caused by overloading or strain

5. Damage to tires and wheels and the loss of or damage to wheel caps unless the motor vehicle is lost or damaged at the same time of accident covered

6. Loss of or damage to goods and/ or personal belongings whilst being loaded unloaded or carried in/ on the motor vehicle

7. Loss or damage to any trailer unless such trailer is specifically declared in the policy schedule

8. Loss or damage to the motor vehicle as a result of theft or any attempt threat due to leaving the motor vehicle in operating mode, leaving the keys therein or non-closing of the doors or screens

9. Radios, stereo equipment, telephones or other accessories other than those originally installed by the vehicle manufacturers and incorporated in the original price of the motor vehicle unless the make and values of such accessories are specifically declared in the schedule

10. Loss or damage caused by using the motor vehicle in unpaved streets or sand hills being driven dangerously or recklessly

11. Being used otherwise than in accordance with the "Limitation as to Use"

12. Carrying passengers in excess of its licensed seating capacity if it is verified that the accident is caused by this breach

13. Being driven by or is for the purpose of being driven by or in the charge of any person other than the Insured or his authorized driver

14. Being used for rallying, racing, pace making, reliability trials, speed testing or being driven dangerously or recklessly

15. Being driven by any person whilst under the influence of intoxicants, drugs or medication which can cause accidents if the vehicle is driven after consuming them

16. Being driven by any person who is less than prescribed age as mentioned in the schedule it may be anywhere between 18 years or 25 years or age. Under age drivers can be covered by amendment.

17. Used within any areas of airports or marine ports, which are not normally accessible to the general public

18. Being used or operated as a tool of trade

19. Being driven by any person who is not holding a driving license or whose driving license is not valid or does not permit him to drive such type of motor vehicle or where such driving license is permanently or temporary cancelled

20. Any liability, which attaches by virtue of an agreement but which would not have attached in the absence of such agreement

Extensions or additional covers to the standard motor insurance policies.

To the above mentioned covers extensions can be provided so as to enhance the coverage. The following are some of the extensions provided to the standard motor policies,

1. Uninsured motorists cover

2. Workmen compensation cover to the driver and passengers

3. Passenger liability cover

4. Personal accident cover to the driver and passengers

5. Medical insurance cover to the driver and passengers

6. Dealer repair option coverage

7. Geographical extension

8. Green card coverage

9. Rent a car reimbursement coverage

10. Emergency medical insurance coverage

11. Protection and removal costs

12. Waiver of depreciation coverage

13. Agreed value coverage

14. Loss of accessories cover

15. Coverage to trailer

1. Uninsured motorist cover

In spite of making the third party liability cover as mandatory many drivers are uninsured or become uninsured due to the conditions of the policy. There may also be hit and run drivers and underinsured drivers, making it impossible to recover the full or partial losses. This results in accidents causing losses which cannot be recovered.

This coverage is usually available in USA and many states are now requiring uninsured motorist coverage in their car insurance policies to help with costs associated with injuries after being involved in a car accident with an uninsured driver.

Drivers also may have the option to purchase uninsured motorist property damage that covers damages to own vehicle and or other property caused by an uninsured driver in an accident.

The uninsured motorists bodily injury covers the driver and the passengers for medical expenses, lost wages, pain and suffering.

Uninsured motorist property damage coverage (UMPD), is also offered by some insurers in United States. It covers loss occurring to the property due to accident caused by uninsured drivers.

2. **Workmen compensation cover to the driver and passengers**

The purpose of providing the insurance under workmen compensation is to make sure that the employees (including the driver on duty) get the statutory compensation as they are not treated as third parties. If extension or additional coverage is provided then they will get compensation as per the workmen compensation acts, which are in force in different countries. The coverage is for the insured's legal liability. The employees of the insured are engaged in the occupation in connection with the vehicle insured or otherwise, that make the insured liable in case of death or injury occurring to the employees. The coverage is for usually the driver, cleaner, laborers and other technicians who travel on the vehicle in the course of employment. Some countries specifically exclude coverage to employees, who are in the course of their employment, under the standard TPL policy. Those countries may recommend this coverage as an optional cover for the benefit of driver and passengers, who are in the course of employment by the insured.

3. Passenger Liability cover

Passengers travelling the vehicle are different types and can be categorized as follows,

- Fare paying passengers

- Non-fare paying passengers

- Driver and Passengers under the contract of employment

The vehicles can be classified as private, commercial and passenger carrying. Some markets treat all passengers as third parties for covering the liabilities. Usually there is a differentiation among the fare paying passengers and non-fare paying passenger. There is also the identification of the driver and passengers (such as cleaners, loaders and other workers) who are coming under the scope of workmen (due to the contract of employment) and passengers, who are not coming under the scope of employment.

The non-fare paying passengers are of two types one who are coming within the scope of employee and the others who are not the employees of the insured. The non-fare paying passengers, who are not the employees of the insured are usually covered under standard TPL coverage without any additional premium. However others who are in the scope of employment of the insured are separately treated as non-fare paying passenger for additional coverage. By paying additional premium per person the insured can cover his employees against liabilities as per law. This is similar to the workmen compensation extension cover as mentioned earlier. However here the passengers, who are covered are not necessarily linked to the vehicle like driver or cleaner. But they are the regular employees of the company travelling from home to work and back or otherwise for some official work in the insured vehicle.

The passenger vehicles (auto-rickshaws, cars, buses, and even two wheelers) will usually carry the passenger for hire and reward, hence they charge money from the passengers. If whilst carrying the passenger any accident occurs and the driver is held responsible then the passenger can claim for damages if any against the driver of the vehicle. This will be covered under the fare paying passenger cover. In some countries this is a compulsory coverage under mandatory third party insurance. By paying the additional premium for each passenger the insured can get a coverage against liability as per the local laws.

In countries where there is no fine differentiation among the passengers inside the vehicle, then the person inside the car other than driver or the insured are treated as third parties and covered under the limits applicable to the TPL schedule of coverage.

4. Personal Accident cover to the Driver and Passengers

This is an additional cover and is an optional cover. It covers death or the injury sustained by the insured or authorized driver and/or any of the passengers as a direct result of an accident to the motor vehicle described in the policy schedule and caused by violent, accidental and visible means which independently of any other cause shall within 52 consecutive weeks of the occurrence of such injury result in death or the covered disability. The coverage for death is usually the standard sum insured in most of the policies, which is usually US $100,000. Other coverage's include total irrevocable loss of all sight in both eyes, which is also the full sum insured i.e., US $100,000. Total loss by physical severance at or above the wrist or ankle of both hands or both feet - US $100,000. Total loss by physical severance at or above the wrist or ankle of one hand or one foot - US $50,000. Total irrevocable loss of all sight in one eye - US $50,000. Permanent disablement from attending any employment or occupation whatsoever is US $100,000. Then there may be cover for weekly benefits of US$ 1,000 per week till 52 weeks or expense incurred in respect of medical and surgical treatment up to US $ 25,000 or may have some other differential coverage.

5. Medical insurance or medical payment coverage to the driver and passengers

This coverage is similar to the personal accident extension coverage. This is also an optional cover and sometimes it is available in place of personal accident cover or in additional to personal accident cover. The premium charged for this coverage may be more than the personal accident coverage.

Medical payments coverage can help cover the medical and or funeral expenses of the drivers and passengers after an accident, regardless of the fault. At an advanced level it will also cover injury as a passenger in someone else's car or even uninsured car. Any car accident outside the car also can be covered.

This may not be very useful if they have full-fledged health insurance plan. The sum insured again varies anywhere from US $10,000 to US$100,000 per person and the premiums are charged accordingly. The coverage includes doctor visits, hospital visits and/or stays, surgery and other relevant medical expenses including prostheses.

There is option to cover only driver or driver along with the passengers. The passengers should be covered up to the legal seating capacity only.

6. <u>Dealer repair option coverage</u>

This is an additional coverage provided to the insured vehicle and it covers the vehicle repair in dealer or agency workshop. There may be restrictions as to the age of the vehicle eligible for the coverage. Vehicles beyond 2 or 3 years are normally not provided with this coverage. The premium charged will be additional premium and there will also be a hike in the deductible.

In the event of damage caused due to an accident then there are two possibilities, either the vehicle is repaired with the dealer or with any other garage or workshop. Normally new cars have warranty and the owners will prefer to repair at the dealers or agency workshop in order to preserve the warranty. Hence this coverage gives them an option to repair the vehicle at any workshop including the dealers workshop. The non-dealer cover does not provide this facility.

7. Geographical extension

Almost all the motor policies have a description of geographical area. The geographical area may be restricted to the part of the country or may be a full state or may be the full country itself. Policies are also issued for the usage of vehicle, restricting to the private area, where there is no access to the public, a discount of between 25 to 50% is allowed in such areas or cases. Any accident occurring outside the geographical area as described in the policy is specifically excluded from the coverage. Hence in order to get a coverage outside the geographical area (outside the country), a separate application need to be made and normally additional premium is charged. The extension is provided to cover basically the own damage cover, as most of the countries have their own laws relating to third party insurances. But in certain cases where there is an agreement or no requirement of mandatory TPL cover to be purchased locally or understanding between the countries about the third party coverage. Then the local insurer can also cover third party coverage in a foreign country. An additional premium is charged for this coverage.

8. Green Card coverage

This is another type of geographical extension. The Green card system is to facilitate the free movement of vehicles over borders and to protect the interests of the victims of foreign registered vehicles.

The Green card is a document which is recognized in many countries and almost all the countries of the Europe. The Green card provides the proof that the minimum legal requirements for third party liability insurance are covered by the insured's own motor policy.

This is suitable for those who are travelling to the countries covered by the countries accepting Green card system. Additional premium is charged for extending this coverage.

9. Rent a car reimbursement coverage

Rental reimbursement or rent a car coverage, is a type of additional car insurance coverage that helps pay for the cost of a rental car while the insured vehicle is being repaired or suffers the loss of use.

Rental reimbursement coverage pays for rental car costs when the vehicle is damaged by one of the perils, which is covered against own damage policy cover.

The insured will be provided with rent a car facility by the insurer and the payments to the rent a car company is done directly by the insurers. In some other cases the insured can take rent a car from the business of his choice and pay for the cost up front. Later on he will submit receipts and a claim form in order to be reimbursed for the cost of the rental vehicle. The coverage of rent a car is not a blanket cover but it comes with a limitation like per day cost and the per accident cost. The Insurance company may provide an inner limit of US $ 50 per day and may be US $ 500 per accident limit or they may put a limit of maximum of 7 to 10 days.

10. <u>Emergency medical insurance coverage</u>

This coverage is for the driver and the passengers in the insured car. If due to any accident the driver and or passengers are injured and need medical treatment then the coverage is provided. The sum insured's are very low, per person limit may range from US $250 to US $1,000. The coverage is inbuilt under most of the package or own damage motor policies and the insurance company does not charge any extra premium for this.

11. <u>Protection and removal costs</u>

This covers the towing, care and protection for insured vehicle. It will bear the reasonable cost of protection and removal to a safe place or the nearest workshop when the motor vehicle is disabled by reason of an accident insured under this policy. There is a monetary limit of coverage for towing usually it is between US$ 500 to US $ 2,000 depending upon the type and size of the vehicle. This coverage is inbuilt in almost all the package or own damage cover policies.

12. Waiver of depreciation coverage

Motor insurance policies are subject to the depreciation clause condition. Wherein a fixed rate of depreciation is enforced at the time of settlement of motor insurance claims. Suppose a new car is purchased for US $ 100,000 and insured for the same amount and it meets with an accident after 9 months, then the insurance company may not pay the full amount. Insurer's will pay the depreciated amount of the car, which may be about 10% or more of the declared value of the car. This will become an issue in case the vehicle is taken on finance. The insured will have to bear the difference in the cost of purchase and the settlement. In such situations the waiver of depreciation is usually helpful. The insurance company will charge additional premium and will provide full coverage. However there are exceptions like tires and batteries etc. This is generally recommended for new vehicles. There is time limitation of from 24 months to 36 months from the first delivery of the vehicle, usually fixed by the insurance companies for application of this endorsement.

13. Agreed value coverage

Motor vehicle policies are based on the insured estimated value (IEV) or insured declared value (IDV), which is usually the market value at the time of insuring the vehicle. In some countries there is availability of a book known as blue book or red book, which provides the values of the vehicles to be insured. However in certain cases the vehicle can also be insured under the special terms known as agreed value. Usually the antique vehicles are insured under this condition. The insured estimated value is agreed by both the insurer and the insured and endorsed in the policy. The coverage usually is good in case of total loss. If due to a covered accident under the policy resulting in partial losses, the usual cost of repair is payable but in case of total loss of the insured vehicle the settlement of the claim is based on the agreed value even though the cost of the vehicle is higher or even lower than the intrinsic value.

14. **Loss of accessories cover**

Loss or damage to accessories fitted in the vehicle such as stereos, fans, air-conditioners etc., it they are not included in the cost of the vehicle. Then they should be covered separately. The extension is provided under the standard vehicle policy to cover the loss of accessories, the property of the Insured specifically declared by them for coverage. Additional premium will be charged to cover accessories.

15. Coverage to trailer

A trailer is an unpowered vehicle pulled by a powered vehicle. Trailers to be used with any vehicle. Each trailer has to be separately identified and covered. Additional premium is charged for covering this type of vehicle against liability coverage or against package coverage.

5. <u>Underwriting in motor insurance</u>

Underwriting is one of the core functions of the insurance company. It is the underwriter, who decides whether a particular risk is acceptable to the company. If he finds the risk is not suitable for underwriting then he will reject the risk. The intention of the underwriter is to avoid adverse selection. Under adverse selection the probability of loss is not factored. However if the underwriter finds the risk as acceptable then he will work-out the premium or rate the risk accordingly and then he will build the terms and conditions suitable to the risk. There may be a detailed process in between the acceptance and rejection. The Underwriter may find certain risk complicated and may seek additional requirements or guarantees before accepting the risk. We can describe **Underwriting as the process of analyzing the risk, determining the premium, other terms and conditions, monitoring the account post acceptance.**

As with other underwriting processes the motor underwriting is simpler and easy to workout. The motor insurance as the terminology it selves is explicit. We should understand the terminology of motor, before trying to insure it. Motor vehicle has been described very clearly in most of the countries, the core definition is that it is a self-propelled vehicle running on motor (machine supplying motive power), and either runs on the tires or chains but does not run on the rails. The traffic law can add up additional parameter for third party mandatory coverage by adding the wording such as "used on public roads". The public liability or third party liability usually arises only when the vehicle or automobile runs on the public road.

Parameters used by the underwriter

The underwriter uses various parameters to underwrite the motor insurance risk. The following are the major parameters used in underwriting,

1. The motor vehicle

2. Usage of the vehicle

3. Insured driver

4. Proposal form

5. Past claims and losses

6. Geographical area of usage

7. Insured estimated value of the vehicle

8. Deductible or excess

9. Safety measures

10. Pre-risk surveys

1. The motor vehicle

Based on the above definition we find many types of vehicles on the road. We may find simple two wheelers (also known by different names such a mopeds, bikes, scooters and motorcycles) or we may find three wheelers also known as auto rickshaws or tuk tuk or simply auto. Then there are four wheelers like cars, jeeps and tempos etc. There are other vehicles which have more than four wheels. These may be trucks, dumpers, haulage vehicles etc. Over-all it is important to know the size and capacity of the vehicle for insurance.

Generally vehicles are categorized into different kinds depending upon its structure and usage. Let us have a look into different categorization of vehicles for the purpose of rating.

 i. Structure and use of the vehicle

 ii. Age of the vehicle

 iii. Color of the vehicle

 iv. Size and capacity of the vehicle

i. Structure and use of the vehicle

Structure and use of vehicle are important element in underwriting. Some type of cars are prone to accidents like Sports utility vehicles are prone to more toppling and pose higher risk than the sedan cars. Bigger cars or vehicles cause higher liabilities in respect of third and own damage risks. Hence the premium charged for bigger vehicles is more.

Depending upon the structure and usage the vehicles are categorized as follows,

 A. Private vehicles

 B. Commercial vehicles

C. Sports Cars

A. **Private vehicles**

The private vehicle is used for personal usage it may be used for social, domestic and pleasure purposes. Usually the individual buys the vehicle either with his own funds or through a financier. The usage is usually for going to office, shopping, dropping and picking the kids from school, visiting places for recreation etc.

Under the private vehicles, based on the structure the following types are popular

- ➢ Motor cycles
- ➢ Private auto rickshaws
- ➢ Private car
- ➢ Other private vehicles
- ➢ High value vehicles

The risk of private vehicle is considered to be better than the commercial vehicle. The private vehicle is usually used either by individuals or juristic entities. But due to its sparse usage the chances of accidents are much lower. Hence the underwriters do a preferential rating for the private vehicles. Even the underwriters are willing to give better terms and less excess or deductible without any extra premium.

B. **Commercial vehicles**

The Commercial vehicles are vehicles used to carry goods or fare paying passengers. The purpose of commercial vehicle is to generate revenue, hence the greater the usage and the greater the speed the revenue generation is higher. Because of the type of usage, more number of accidents are occurring to the commercial vehicles. From the point of view of insurers, in respect of overall portfolio the commercial vehicle generate more premium than the personal or sports vehicles. As far as the rating is concerned, it is more complex than the private vehicles. The underwriter again differentiates groups within the commercial vehicles for underwriting purposes. The underwriter also uses the computer or smart systems to aid him in rating the commercial risks.

Under the commercial vehicles, once again based on the structure the following types are popular

➤ Motor cycles

➤ Commercial auto rickshaws

➤ Commercial cars

➤ Other commercial vehicles

Based on the usage some of the vehicles (the list is not exhaustive) can be classified as follows,

➤ Goods carrying vehicles

➤ Fare paying passenger vehicles

- Ambulances
- Trailers
- Reefers
- Pneumatic vehicles
- Flatbed haulage trucks
- Light commercial vehicles
- Heavy commercial vehicles
- Medium commercial vehicles
- Buses
- Mini buses
- Van
- Coaches
- Tipper
- Dumper
- Bobcat
- Poclain
- Towing vehicles

C. Sports cars

Sports cars are different cars and are specially designed to run at high speed. The prices of the cars are usually higher. The repair cost of these cars are very costly. Hence it requires separate underwriting. Unless there are some compulsions or business requirement, majority of the underwriters prefer to decline this type of risk. The underwriter makes sure that the sum insured of the vehicle is within his authority as most of the insurance companies restrict the underwriting limit of the underwriter in case of sports cars. The own damage and damage to the third parties are tremendous due to high speed of these vehicles. Moreover the users of these vehicles are usually youngsters. Apart from higher rates the underwriter also increase the deductibles.

ii. Age of the vehicle

Age of the vehicle is an important factor for underwriters especially whilst writing a package policy. The third party insurance may not be much problem. But most of the companies have guidelines for underwriting vehicles for package policy. One of the main reasons of these guidelines is the principle of indemnity, which states that the insured should be in the similar condition after the loss as he was before the loss. Hence if an old vehicle is insured and the insurance company pays the claim without taking into consideration the depreciation in parts then it will be a violation of principle of indemnity. The underwriter will not be interested to underwrite a vehicle which is more than 5 years old. However he may insist upon various conditions like inspection of the vehicle especially for personal lines insurance. Personal line insurance is the insurance of vehicles belonging to the individuals usually private vehicles. He may also incorporate certain condition like depreciation clause and higher deductible to safeguard the interest of the insurance company. In most of the cases the underwriters are not willing to insure a vehicle beyond 7 to 10 years under package insurance policy.

iii. Color of the vehicle

In most of the markets around the world color of the vehicle does not play an important role in underwriting. However in certain advanced countries due to availability of huge amount of statistics, it has been found that the red color cars are more prone to accident and this is taken into consideration whilst underwriting the red color cars.

iv. Size and capacity of the vehicle

Size and capacity of the vehicle is also an important consideration for underwriting purposes. The commercial vehicles are classified based on the size like light commercial vehicle, medium commercial vehicle or heavy commercial vehicle. They also may be classified based on the tonnage. Cars are usually categorized based on the horsepower or cubic centimeters or liters. Passenger carrying vehicles are based on the manufacturers specified seating capacity like 8 seater, 30 seater and 55 seater etc. One of the criteria used for rating is based on the classification of vehicle based on the size and capacity of the vehicle.

2. Usage of the vehicle

The usage of the vehicle is very important underwriting criteria. If the vehicle is used for commercial purposes then the rating is higher.

In commercial vehicles also we may have tankers which carry liquid. If the tanker is used to carry water then the exposure to loss is less than compared to a tanker carrying hazardous chemicals or explosive material. Hence the underwriter is particularly concerned about the usage of the vehicle.

Similarly if we look into the passenger carrying vehicles. If the vehicles are used within the city the chances of accidents are less even if there are accidents the exposure is less compared to the vehicles which are being driven on the country side as the distances are long and the driver may not get adequate rest and will be forced to drive even during nights and at high speed. This will definitely result in high cost associated with the accidents happening to such vehicles. The underwriter will have to examine such situations carefully and rate the risks accordingly.

Even within the same category of vehicles the higher the mileage the higher the depreciation and higher the chances of accident. A private vehicle which is supposed to be safer can be rated differently based on the usage of the vehicle. For example Mr. A has a Toyota Camry, 2014 model and Mr. B also has a Toyota Camry 2014 model both cars are purchased by them on the same date and at the same price. But the kilometer running of Mr. A's car is 250,000 whereas the kilometer running of the Mr. B's car is 24,000. The kilometer running can be easily found if we look into the Odometer. On further exploration it was found that Mr. A is driving to his office which is over 50 kilometers and he is also dropping his wife and kids to their office and schools respectively. Apart from that he is from countryside and he travels weekly to his home town. This definitely will create a bigger exposure to Mr. A than compared to Mr. B, who drives from home to office and back. On weekends he goes for shopping. The usage of Mr. A is almost 10 times more than that of Mr. B. Hence the underwriter will be charging more premium to Mr. A compared to Mr. B or will end up loading more deductible to Mr. A.

The role of underwriter is to identify the correct usage of the vehicle and incorporate the same in the policy. Any violation of the usage can make the policy null and void.

The maintenance of the vehicle is also important a well maintained car is a good risk whereas a badly maintained car poses a morale hazard and may lead to a major loss.

3. Insured driver

Driver is also an important parameter in underwriting. The best car, if driven by a bad driver will result in accidents and losses. Hence the underwriter will take into account lot of information related to the Driver.

The age of the driver has a bearing on the loss ratio. The younger drivers are prone to make accidents and cause losses. The younger drivers are more enthusiastic and easy to make bad decisions which will end up in accident and loss.

Age of the driving license and the years of experience of driving a motor vehicle. A holder of new driving license is considered a high risk. Apart from this the insured might have obtained a driving license but did not get an opportunity to drive hence the age of driving license may be more but the experience may be less. The underwriter must get the detailed information in order to understand the real experience of the driver in driving the vehicle.

The underwriters should also know whether the driver is suffering from any physical and or mental infirmity, hearing problems or defective vision or even color blindness. These attributes will have impact on the accidents. The healthy and physically fit drivers will have more endurance and will cause less accidents compared to the person with some of the defects as mentioned above.

The sex of the driver may also be a criteria for underwriting. Studies have been done on this issue and it has been found that the women are much safer drivers compared to the men. Once again this is not the major criteria for underwriting.

Apart from the age of the driver some even consider marital status, which has a bearing on the risk. There is an assumption that most married people tend to stay at home compared to the bachelors. This assumption makes married people as safer risk compared to the bachelors.

Driver past accident records also help in making a right underwriting decision. If a driver has more number of accidents then the chances are that he may be a bad driver or a careless driver. The careless driver reflect a morale hazard. Hence he should be rated higher and even the deductible can be increased.

Occupation and educational level of the driver is also important as there are certain occupations which have proven to have bad accident records. Even driver with good education seems to be good drivers. Some insurance companies treat these as important underwriting criteria for motor insurance.

Conviction of driver for traffic violations is also an important criteria for evaluating the risk the underwriter is assuming. A person with numerous conviction will be a morale hazard and may cause a loss to the insurance company. The underwriter should be able to probe the detailed information obtained with regard to convictions normally during the last five years.

4. Proposal form

A proposal form is an important document in insurance and it is the most important part of the Insurance contract. The proposal form is treated as an offer from the insured to buy the insurance policy. The proposal form contains all the details related to the insured, insured vehicle and the driver etc.

The proposal form may be a single sheet A4 size paper to a multiple page booklet containing lot of information related to the material facts and the regulatory requirements and the contact information.

The motor proposal form contains various sections. Some of the major sections of the proposal form are as follows,

   i. Insured related section

   ii. Vehicle related section

   iii. Driver related section

   iv. Coverage and Benefits section

   v. Miscellaneous section

   vi. Declaration section

i.   **Insured related section**

Insured related information section usually contains the information pertaining to the insured, like his name, address, his business or occupation, telephone numbers, fax numbers, email and other contact information. Other information will relate to bankruptcy or insolvency, whether any insurer has declined his proposal or any insurer has imposed any additional terms and conditions to the policy. The questions may also relate to any financial interest in the vehicle being insured.

ii.   Vehicle related section

Vehicle related information section will contain vehicle make, model, identification numbers, registration numbers, year of manufacture, color of the vehicle, engine capacity, weight of the vehicle, seating capacity, usage of the vehicle, whether any alteration has been done to the vehicle from the manufacturers specification, and insured estimate of the value (IEV) or also known as insured declared value (IDV) of the vehicle. These are some of the major questions asked by the underwriter through the proposal form for evaluation purpose. The IEV or the IDV is the sum insured under the policy.

iii.   Driver related section

Driver related information section contains the following information related to the drivers, his name, date of birth, occupation, date of license, any physical or mental infirmity of the driver including defective sight and hearing, convictions during last five years, past loss and past claims experience (claims history) during the last five years. In most of the commercial vehicle insurance or fleet insurance, there is a turnover of drivers, hence it is difficult to get the right details of the driver. Hence in such situations the fleet safety program of the organization will be useful.

iv.   Coverage and benefits section

Coverage section will allow the insured to choose the type of covers and the benefits he would like to have. The period of coverage will allow the insured to provide the date of the inception and expiry of the coverage. Like whether he would like to go in for the third party only coverage or would like to take a package policy.

Apart from this, what additional benefit covers he will be willing to go in for like personal accident cover to the driver and the passengers, dealer repair option cover or extension of the geographical limit cover etc.

v.   Miscellaneous section

This section may contain different requirements like payment area (in case payment is by credit card, the necessary details to be filled in). Acceptance area, which will allow the underwriter to put in his remarks as to the acceptance and other terms and conditions. Disclosure of material fact area, which will reiterate the importance of material fact and warn the consequences of not disclosing the material fact.

vi.   Declaration section

Declaration section will contain the declaration by the insured that the information provided by him is true and complete to the best of his knowledge and it will also contain information about the material fact and the instruction as to what is a material fact and what type of fact need to be disclosed.   The final portion of the declaration will contain signature of the insured, name of the signatory and date of on which it is singed.

5. Past claims and losses

The past claims and losses are a good indication of what can be expected in the future. Hence it has to be thoroughly evaluated by the underwriter. The underwriter uses this information for rating the risk. Some risks like the fleet risks are sometime rated based solely on the past claims and losses data. There is a small deference between the past claims and the past losses. Data related to the past claims can be obtained from the past insurer or insurers, whereas the data related to the past losses can only be provided by the insured. There is a possibility that the claims can be lower than the deductible which has not been claimed by the insured from the insurance company. Such losses also will play an important role in rating the risk and providing the necessary terms and conditions.

Claims experience is usually taken separately for the third party and own damage sections. This gives a true picture for rating. Usually the underwriters ignore one off large loss so that the insured is not penalized for such a loss whilst rating.

6. Geographical area of usage

Some insurance companies have differential rating for different geography. Like a vehicle plying on the city roads is considered at a higher risk than a vehicle plying on the countryside. Then the underwriters also categorize areas of risk, like the vehicle when used near a sea coast is more prone to rusting and may cause more accident and depreciation than the vehicles which are used in the places away from the sea side. Similarly some areas are prone to natural disasters like floods. The rating for vehicles coming from such areas may have higher compared to the vehicles coming from other safe areas. There are also areas prone to theft and some areas are considered safer areas. The areas which are prone to theft will invite additional premium and a higher deductible the areas which are considered safer.

7. Insured estimated value or sum insured of the vehicle

Insured estimated value (IEV) also known as the Insured declared value (IDV) is an important requirement of motor insurance. IEV becomes sum insured under own damage section of the vehicle. It is required for package policies. This is not required for the third party insurance. The rating for the vehicle is based on the IEV and the underwriters usually work out a percentage of the IEV and if the value is low then there is a minimum premium criteria which will take care of low value cars. This value is provided by the insured and the insurer will only make as judgment as to the correctness of the value. The declaration of low value will go against the insured. Whereas declaring a higher value than the real price of the vehicle will cause the insured to pay more premium without any benefit.

For example if Mr. X want to insure his car which is worth US$ 100,000 and the underwriter decides to rate it at 4% then the insurer will charge 4% of 100,000 which comes to

US $ 4,000. The insurer has a minimum premium criteria at US $1,000. In another case if Mr. Y wants to insure his car and the IDV or IEV is US $ 20,000 and the rate arrived by the underwriter is 4%. Then based on the value the premium should come to US$ 800. But in view of minimum premium criteria the premium charged to the insured will be US $1,000, which is the minimum premium criteria.

8. **Deductible or excess**

Deductible or excess are one and same, the dictionary meaning may be slightly different but the overall meaning in insurance is one and same. Most of the insurers use it synonymously. The underwriter will impose a minimum compulsory deductible under the policy known as compulsory excess. However the insured does not have choice to reduce the compulsory excess but he has a choice to increase the excess and get a discount in the rates from the insured. If insured is a good driver and feels that he may not be able to make accidents, then he will increase the excess in the hope of getting the discount in the premium rate. The deductible opted by the insured is known as the voluntary deductible. The underwriter will have twin benefit if the insured is opting for the voluntary deductible. He will save the claims cost and the claims administration costs. This will allow him to make the discount to the insured. Thus this will help both the insured and the insurance company in reducing the costs.

For example in the above case if Mr. X wants to insure his car then the insurer will offer him a deductible of US $ 500 each and every claim. This deductible is compulsory and the insured cannot get a deductible less than US $ 500. However if Mr. X is a safe driver and he would like to avail some benefit then he can go in for reduction in premium by increase the deductible. Suppose he would like to volunteer for a higher deductible of US $ 1,500. Then he may get a discount in rating, usually the underwriter is willing to reduce the premium by half a percent. The rating for the risk will be revised from 4% to 3.5%. Mr. X will be paying a premium of US $ 3,500 for going for a higher voluntary deductible of US $ 1,500.

9. Safety measures

Technological advances has helped in building features in the vehicles that will protect the passengers and also the vehicle from accidental damages and thefts. Vehicle technology has helped the insurers track the running of the vehicle, it has also given the insured the navigational tools and other feature like sensors to avoid the accident to the vehicle. The features like air-bags, seat belts and strong body of the vehicle help in protecting the driver and the passengers. Other features like designing of the vehicle so as to make it more stable on the road and in case of accident. The built in cameras and sensors help in avoiding minor as well as major accidents. A theft alarm and steering wheel lock will help in preventing losses due to theft. The insurance industry is hopeful of many new features being brought into the vehicle to avoid accidents and to reduce the losses. The underwriter need to consider these feature while underwriting a vehicle risk. Under fleet insurance the underwriter should take into consideration the fleet safety program. A fleet safety program should have the right processes and procedures to help improve safety and reduce costs. All the stakeholders should be involved in the process. The Insurance company representative can also become a part of the fleet safety program. The underwriter will discount the standard rates in case the insured has safety features in his risk.

10. Pre-Risk surveys

Pre-risk surveys one of the important element of underwriting. In most of the individual or personal lines risks or small commercial risks the pre-risk surveys are recommended to avoid fraud and make sure that the risk is acceptable. It is almost essential in case of high risk groups like hazardous tankers, haulage trucks or chemical carrying vehicles etc. The pre-risk survey can be done by the in-house representative or can be outsourced to a third party loss adjuster or surveyor. The in-house surveys are done by the salesman of the insurance company or the underwriter or one of their claims staff. However in case of commercial fleet the outside surveyor is used. The outside surveyor is a professional will be able to provide the full scale details of the risk being insured. The main purpose of the pre-risk surveys is to obtain the full description of the risk being insured and assess the physical and other hazards of the risk. It will also help in understanding the correctness of the proposal form. A professional pre-risk survey especially related to a commercial risk will also suggest risk improvement and loss prevention measures. The outside agency will provide the photographs of the risk along with the pre-risk survey report.

<u>Process of underwriting</u>

The following are some of the steps involved in the process of underwriting.

- Obtaining the necessary Information

- Understanding the risks involved

- Rating the risk

- Endorsements

- Warranties

- Quotation

- Monitoring the Underwritten risks

Obtaining the necessary information

It is one of the important aspect of underwriting. The required information can be provided by the prospect directly or it can be provided by the Agent or Broker. One of the easiest way of getting the information is through the proposal form. The proposal form is a simple document and is used to extract the material information from the client. It along with other documents form the complete insurance contract. Any misrepresentation in the proposal may lead to the denial of liability by the insurer and will allow the insurer to treat the contract as null and void.

Understanding the risks involved

Once the necessary underwriting information is gathered by the underwriter. He will analyze the information obtained for the purpose of the insuring the vehicle or fleet. The underwriter will evaluate the perils need to be covered and the hazards which are coming with the risk or the motor vehicle of the area of operation or the type of business or other parameters. After getting the necessary information the underwriter can take three decision. He may straightaway decline to insure the risk or he may straightaway accept the risk as presented to him. The third option may be he may ask for further information related to the risk before he can take a suitable decision. After getting the additional information the underwriter has a right to accept the risk or reject the risk. Once a decision is taken by the underwriter to accept the risk, his priority is to calculate the premium or the rate for insuring the risk and workout the suitable terms and conditions applicable to the policy.

The information required may be different for the different type of risk. We can categorize the risks into the following types.

- Personal lines (covering Private vehicles)

- Commercial Lines or Corporate business (Covering the vehicles belonging to the businesses such as private sector and public sector including the business from the Government)

Personal lines

Personal lines business is coming out of the individuals who are owning the vehicles. The information needed for personal lines motor insurance may come through the simple proposal form, copies of vehicle registration and driving license. Usually an inspection report is also insisted upon by most of the insurers depending upon the type of customer. The inspection is usually done by the in-house representative. However for the third party insurance the inspection of the vehicle is not mandatory. The insurance company can take their own precaution like insuring from the date and time of acceptance or providing coverage after a lapse of certain time period after the receipt of the premium along with the other underwriting requirements.

Commercial lines

The risks under the commercial lines business is bit complex and it covers a whole array of vehicles. The insurance policies designed for and bought by businesses, individuals or juristic persons are usually termed as commercial lines. Individuals using vehicles for commercial purposes are also treated as commercial lines. These risks are usually further classified such as small, medium and large accounts or markets respectively. The vehicles may be from simple two wheelers to a complex mobile crane and huge haulage trucks.

Usually under commercial lines there may be need for additional information. Some insurance companies do not require the proposal form, whereas other may ask for simplified proposal form. The prospect should also provide details about the past claims experience and the vehicle schedules in soft copy. The soft copy will make it easier to classify the vehicles for rating purpose and in case of usage of smart systems it will be useful for generating the required data quickly. In case the broker is involved then the broker slip may provide the necessary information needed by the insurer to underwrite the risk. The insurance company may ask for fleet or commercial risk control report. This report can be prepared by the in-house expert or can be outsourced. The report will provide details of the risk after the physical inspection by the representative of the insurer or the third party risk surveyor. Under commercial lines risk, there is a huge variation like passenger carrying vehicles, goods carrying vehicles, special type of vehicles. Some vehicles linked to the garages and showrooms can be covered under motor trade risk cover, which is a very special cover under the motor policy and covers road risks, road transit risk and internal risks. There are commercial vehicles used as tools of trade (tool or plant is attached to the vehicle for performing the necessary function), in general terms the liability and damage to the motor vehicle is excluded under the policy. However there is a provision to include the coverage by way of tools of trade endorsement. The underwriter will charge an additional premium for amending the policy or may suggest it to be covered under public liability and plant and equipment covers separately.

Rating the Risk

There are various methods of rating the risks based on the information obtained by the underwriter, some of the methods are as follows,

- Book rate

- Tariff rate

- Rating through smart systems

- Experience rating

- Judgmental rating

- Business decision rating

Book rate

Some insurance companies may have their own underwriting manual which guide the underwriters for writing the risk. The manuals may provide the base rate or we can also name it as the book rate structure and the underwriter based on the other parameters will make adjustments to the base rate to arrive at the net rate. For good features the underwriter gives discounts and for bad features he may load the premiums.

For example the rating of a private motor vehicle is 4% as per the book maintained by the motor insurance underwriter. The book states that if the vehicle is in operation the city with a population of 500,000 then the rate to be loaded by 10%. It the insured opts for voluntary deductible or US $ 5,000 then the rate can be reduced by 25%. Good features like theft guard will allow a discount of 5% from the rating. Suppose Mr. X wants to insure his car work 100,000 and it is being operated in New York city then the underwriter will take the book rate of 4% and load it by 10% to make it 4.4% and rate the risk accordingly. The new premium will work out to US $ 4400 instead of a standard rate of US $ 4,000. Similarly if he is opting for a voluntary deductible of US $ 5,000 then he is entitled for a discount of 25% on the revised rate. The underwriter will recalculate the rate by allowing the necessary discount. After discount the rate comes to 3.3%. This revise the premium to US $ 3,300. Similarly other terms are also scaled as per the needs and quality of the risk.

Tariff

Some countries may have tariff rating system, it is usually prescribed by a tariff body, which is set by an advisory body and it becomes mandatory for the members to follow the rates prescribed in the tariff. The members are not allowed to breach the rates prescribed by the tariff. This was a mandatory system of rating for motor insurance in India prior to privatization of insurance. Tariff system is also used in other classes of insurance.

Rating through smart systems

This can be done semi automatically or fully with the aid of computerized programs also known as the smart systems. The program may give the rating along with the conditions to be incorporated into the policy. All the required information related to the risk has to be fed into the system in order to get the correct output. Smart Systems is a great tool in the hands of a good underwriter. It provides a number of combinations to help him arrive at the right rating structure and get the right terms and conditions before incorporating the same into the quotation.

Experience rating

Experience rating is one of the traditional methods of rating. In this methodology rating of the risk is based on the past claims experience of the risk. This methodology is suitable for a fleet of vehicles. In this type of rating the premium is scaled up and down to reflect the insured loss experience during the part period. A risk with good experience gets a good rating, whereas an account with bad experience gets higher premium and higher deductibles. There is an assumption that a good performing account will continue to perform good and yield good results. One of the common method of experience rating is the "burning cost method". Under this the ratio of losses and premium required to cover the same is worked out in order to arrive at a suitable rate.

Judgmental rating

Judgmental rating is usually done for personal lines and small accounts, where there is lack of sufficient information and the underwriter is generally satisfied with the risk being insured he will go in for judgmental rating. However in this type of rating the underwriter should be careful so that he does not go below the minimum rates required to sustain the risk, he should also remember the requirement of the minimum premium required for each risk.

Business decision rating

In certain markets there may not be much maneuverability, but the underwriter may be forced to take a business decision. We define business decision as "A decision taken to secure a business, to get the goodwill of the business or the market. The ultimate goal of the decision is to procure more business from the customer and the market". The customary rate of the insurer is usually discounted to secure the business.

From the underwriting point of view the simplest underwriting is for third party insurance followed by the personal lines insurance. In motor third party insurance the rates are usually fixed and are non-negotiable. Almost all the countries in the World have the mandatory third party motor insurance. Hence the coverage is usually standardized, this also leads to the standardization of the rates and the underwriting process. The rates are based on the experience of the insurer and the overall experience of the market. The rating may be decided by the insurer and in most of the markets the ratings have to be approved by the regulators. Under personal lines insurance the insurer may have go by the base rate and then look into other parameters and work out a net rate which is easy to compile with. Whereas in the fleet polices the underwriter has to first classify the vehicles and then segregate the losses under each section and then rate them accordingly. The underwriter will also decide about the deductible and usually he will have a compulsory deductible and usually the deductible is different for different types of risks like in the personal lines insurance it will be least for the two wheelers and it will be highest for the sports cars. The commercial vehicles will also have a higher deductible.

The other important elements of the underwriting process are as follows,

- Endorsements

- Warranties

- Quotations

Endorsements

Broadly speaking and in practice endorsements are also known as amendments to the policy. If we look very finely then there will be difference between amendment and the endorsement. In most of the markets they are used interchangeably. In case of conflict between the policy schedule and the endorsement the endorsement will override the policy schedule. Based on the information provided and the coverage requirements, the underwriter will identify different endorsements for different types risks. Like if one customer is opting for an additional deductible. Then the underwriter will incorporate the endorsement pertaining to the voluntary deductible and reduce the premiums accordingly. The insured may request for geographical extension or personal accident benefits to the passenger and the driver. Even for these the underwriter will price the product and then will incorporate the necessary endorsements. If the new vehicle is purchased by the insured and the same need to be added to the policy. In such a situation the insured will advise the insurance company and they will add the vehicle to the policy by way of endorsement to the policy.

Warranties

Warranties are also used by the underwriter. A warranty is a text incorporated by the insurer, binding the insured with a promise to the insurer to maintain certain features or refrain from certain features of the risk. It is the important condition of the policy and goes to the heart of the policy. Noncompliance of warranty may deny the claim. In certain cases the underwriter may put some warranties to make sure that the insured follows them properly in order to prevent the losses. The underwriter may put a warranty as to the minimum age of the driver or the maintenance of the vehicle. Example of a warranty for underage driver can be as "It is hereby declared and warranted that the vehicle will not be driven by a driver, who is under the age of 21 years". This will help the underwriter from the adverse effects of the risk. The underwriter need not worry or contest the insured but make sure that warranty is complied with and make sure that the risk is as per his rating throughout the policy period.

Quotations

Once the rating, endorsements and warranties are finalized then the underwriter will prepare a quotation for covering the risk. The quotation can be verbal or written. The underwriter must make sure that the quotation is done correctly as it will become a part of the contract and should not promise something which cannot be covered under the policy. If insured accepts the quotation provided by the insurance company or the underwriter then it becomes a contract. The insured has to pay the premium as agreed. The premium is the consideration of the contract. The insurer will promise to make good the financial loss occurring during the period of insurance due to a covered peril and as per the terms and conditions of the policy. The motor insurance premium is calculated on an annual basis. The premium paid is not refundable at the end of the year even if there is no claim during the policy period. The premium is observed as the cost of the promise made by the insurer for one year. Hence the money is not refundable unlike life insurance. However if the insured wants to cancel the policy mid-term then the premium is refunded on short-period basis. **Short period basis** means in case of cancellation of the policy the refund of the premium is not proportionate to the number of days left in the policy. The premium charged to the insured is higher than the proportionate premium and refund premium is lower than the proportionate premium. If the insurance company decides to cancel the policy of the insured then the insurance company usually provide a pro-rata refund of the premium. In **pro-rata refund** of premium, in case of cancellation of the policy mid-term the insured will get the refund of premium on a proportionate basis. The premium charged by the insurer and the premium refunded to insured is proportionate.

Monitoring the underwritten risks

The underwriter's job does not end with the acceptance of the insurance. The process continues and he has to carefully monitor all the risks he has insured. If he finds problems with any of the risks then he should make sure to remedy the situation. If underwriter finds any risk having many claims then he should make a thorough enquiry and then make the necessary remedial measures like putting additional warranties or increasing the deductible or even cancelling the policy altogether.

The overall goal of an underwriter is to make reasonable underwriting profit for the organization.

6. <u>Motor claims settlement</u>

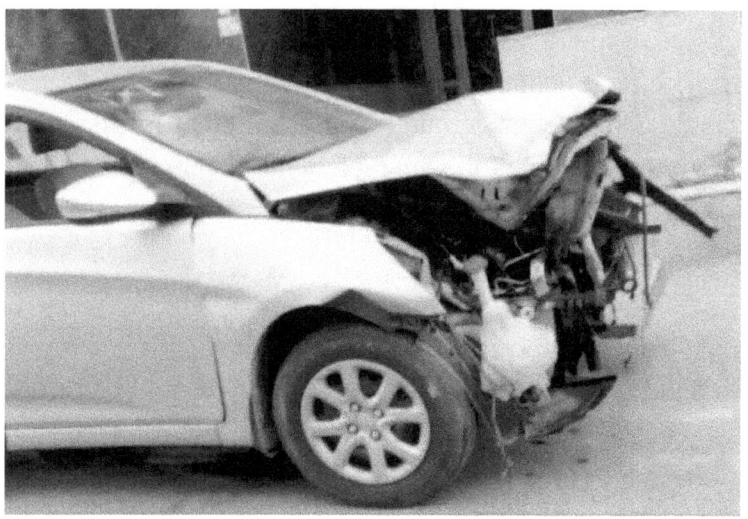

Claims settlement is the other core function, post underwriting of the insurance companies. In insurance contract premium is the consideration paid by the insured to get the insurance coverage. Whereas the consideration on part of insurance company is the promise to pay the covered claim as per the terms of the policy. Claim settlement is the fulfillment of the promise made to the insured. Practically the insurance company is only providing a document when the agreement is finalized. The actual cost of documentation may be between US $10 to US $ 100. But the promise of coverage may run into millions. The customer is only able to gauge the service of the insurance company only at the time of the settlement of the claim. Motor insurance is one of the attrition class of business. Hence the frequency of claims under motor insurance is high. However the severity of claims is considerably low.

In case of motor vehicle accident the insured has to comply with certain requirements and the insurance company also should comply with certain requirements. The insured need to comply with the following guidelines in case of accident leading to valid claim.

Insured duties

First and the foremost in case of accident the insured should report to the police and other relevant authorities and comply with their requirements.

The insured should not leave the vehicle unattended or unlocked, as any theft of car parts or accessories thereafter will not be covered under the policy.

The insured should avoid any kind of repairs on the vehicle without the knowledge of the insurance company.

Should not do any action which may cause further damage to the vehicle suppose in an accident the oil is completely leaked then driving the vehicle without oil will damage the engine. Hence the driving should be avoided.

If any third party is involved in the accident the insured should not admit his liability under any circumstances, even if the insured is at fault.

The insured should also obtain the following details of the third party.

- The owner's name, address and telephone number.

- If the vehicle is being driven then the driver's name and his address.

- The name of the owner's insurance company, if any.

- The make, type and registration number of the vehicle.

- The name and address of witnesses, if any.

- The insured also should record the date, time and location of the accident.

- Should also provide his own policy number to the insurance company.

If the claim is above the excess limit or the insured wants to lodge a claim with the insurance company then he has to notify the insurance company or the broker or his office (if the client is a corporate customer). The insured need to inform the insurance company at the earliest opportunity. Some insurance companies will fix a time limit for the notification of claim after accident as delay in notification will give scope for fraud and even denial of the claim.

In motor insurance, claims can be classified into the following three types

- Third party claims or liability claims

- Own damage claims or first party claims

- Miscellaneous claims

Third party claims or liability claims

The third party claims arises when the accident is caused by the fault of the insured driver. The third party claims can be of two types.

- Third party death or bodily injury

- Third Party property damage

Third party death or bodily injury

If the person dies or injured due to the fault or negligence of the insured driver, then there is a potential for third party death or bodily injury claim. The person or persons who can be injured are categorized as follows,

- Persons inside the vehicle other than driver

- Persons outside the vehicle

Persons inside the vehicle other than driver

The persons inside the vehicle can be family, friends, relative or known and unknown persons. There may also be commercial situation like fare paying passengers, non-fare paying passengers, employees and contractors. All these people are treated as third party for the purpose of claim. However in some cases the employees are excluded from the definition of the third party and they are covered under workmen compensation claim.

Persons outside the vehicle

All the persons who are not inside the car are treated as persons outside the car. The people who are outside the car will include pedestrians, people travelling in other vehicles, people sleeping on the road or people in their residences and or offices.

Third party property damage

Any loss or damage caused to the property belonging to the third parties is covered under the third party section of the policy. The most common of third party property damage claims are damage caused to other vehicles by the insured vehicle.

Any other properties other than cars is also covered under the motor third party insurance. If the insured is held responsible for the loss under a covered policy then his claim become admissible.

Own damage or first party claims

Any claims arising out of loss of or damage to the insured vehicle is termed as own damage claim, earlier it was also known as first party claim. These claims may arise either due to the fault of the insured driver or due to fault of third party driver or may be due to other causes also like the natural calamities or unknown vehicle. The claims arising out under the own damage claims are classified into two as follows,

- Partial loss claims

- Total loss claims

Partial loss claims

Partial losses are said to occur when the vehicle which meets with an accident is repairable. The repair can restore the vehicle look similar to as it was before the accident. The repair can be done with replaceable parts or without parts. The insurance company will identify the labor cost for repairing the vehicle and if required the cost of the material and parts for repairing the vehicle. Based on the estimate and actual cost of repair the settlement is made. The settlement is done for both the spare parts and the labor charges. Where necessary a depreciation is applied and the amount is deducted from the claim. The final claim is net of deductible.

Total Loss claims

Total loss claims will allow the insurer's to write off the vehicle and settle the claim to the insured. Total loss claims can be settled by asking the insured to retain the salvage or deducting the estimated cost of the salvage. Value derived from the damaged property is known as salvage. If the claim is settled by insurance company and the insured retains the salvage then the settlement is less complicated. In case the insurance company retains the salvage then the insured should surrender the original vehicle ID and also standard documents, which are required by the local registration authority for transfer of the salvage. One of the important aspect of the total loss settlement is the amount of claim, which is payable to the insured. Usually the insurance companies restrict the claims payment by a condition which states that in case of total loss the claim settlement is restricted to the sum insured or the market value, whichever is less. In this type of loss also the deductible is applied. The total loss claims are of two types

- Standard total loss claims

- Constructive total loss claims

Standard total loss claims

Under this type of total loss the insurer will assess the cost of repairing the vehicle and will also look into the salvage aspect of the vehicle. After obtaining the accurate data related to the repairing the insurer will check if the cost of repairing the vehicle including parts and other consumables are higher than the value of the vehicle, if it is found that the cost of repair exceeds the value of the vehicle or the sum insured under the policy then the insurance company will go for settlement of the claim on total loss basis. In some cases if the cost of repairing the vehicle exceed 75% of the IEV or IDV, then the insurance company may treat the claim as a total loss claim. This condition may be in form of written condition or may be implied as per the market norms.

Constructive total loss claims

Whenever a loss occurs and the cost of repairing the damaged vehicle and the cost of salvage is same or more than the market value or the sum insured of the vehicle, it is treated as constructive total loss.

Miscellaneous claims

There are other claims other than the third party and own damage claims and these are coming under the miscellaneous claims. The most common miscellaneous claims are as follows,

- Personal accident claim

- Emergency medical expenses claim

- Workmen compensation or legal liability claim.

Personal accident claim

The coverage provided under the motor insurance policy is usually restricted cover. It provides coverage in respect of death, loss of limbs and loss of eye. It also provides coverage in respect of permanent total disablement. Few covers are also available in the market which will provide cover for weekly benefit under temporary total disablement. These claims are lodged separately and have a separate claim form. The requirements for these type of claims are different like medical report, police report and a report from a third opinion doctor.

Emergency medical expenses claim

The intention is to provide a very small amount of coverage to each passenger and the driver in the car. It usually covers to a limit of anywhere between US $ 100 to US $ 500. The coverage is provided only when the damage is caused due to direct and immediate result of an accident to the motor vehicle covered under the policy.

Workmen compensation claim.

The standard policies are usually extended to cover the claims arising under the workmen compensation regulations. It usually covers the drivers, cleaners and other employees of the insured who travel in the vehicle as part of duty or employment. Most of the persons are employed by the insured in the operation and maintenance of the motor vehicle.

Damages or Claims

Any accident may result in the death or injury to the third parties. The claim is decided based on various factors including the age, occupation, gender and income of the person injured or dead. The damages are usually awarded by the Court. The damages are the money recoverable by the victim from the party responsible for death or injury. The damages can be categorized into the following,

- General damages

- Specific damages

- Punitive damages

General damages

General damages flow naturally from the party responsible for the wrongful action. The value of general damages cannot be measured financially. It is the compensations sought for the pain and suffering, mental agony, loss of healthy life, loss of opportunity and leading a low quality life. The award for these damages are generally on a case by case basis hence it will be difficult to benchmark these losses. These are usually occurring in the third party personal injury claims.

Specific damages

These are usually measureable financially. These damages can be documented and are easy to assess. In case of hospitalization it is easy to know the cost of treatment. The loss is based on the treatment cost. Whereas in case damage to the bumper the cost of bumper is known and the cost of replacing the bumper is also known. Hence the insured will be in a position to submit the claim with the necessary vouchers and bill in order to claim the award. A vast majority of motor claims come under the specific damage claims.

Punitive damages

Punitive damages are financial compensation awarded to an injured party. It is over and above the normal compensation and the purpose is to punish the party at fault. Almost all the insurance policies do not cover these types of damages. Covering punitive damages under the insurance policy will encourage the people to become more reckless and commit gross misconduct. Hence the insured is left uninsured as far as the punitive damage cover is concerned. The insured has to pay the cost of punitive damage to the concerned authority or the third party.

Motor Insurance Claims process

Each insurance company has its own system of processing of the claims. However the general process performed by the insurance companies in respect of motor claims are as follows,

- Receipt of claim notice from the insured

- Acknowledgement of the claim

- General requirements and documentations for Third party claims

- Claim registration

- Building rapport with the customer

- Claim assessment and investigations

- Settlement options

- Final settlement of the claim

- Post claim settlement process

Receipt of claim notice from the insured

The insurance company as soon as it receive the claim notification from the insured has to respond to the insured as per the regulatory requirement or as per their internal standards. On receipt of the claim intimation the insurance company will make the necessary checks as to validity of the claim, the payment of premium, adequacy of the coverage, the validity of the policy, insurable interest, estimate of loss etc. Once the claim is found to be in order the insurance company will proceed to the next step.

Acknowledgement of the claim

The insurance company may assign the claim to its claims supervisor or claims representative. The insurance claims representative will immediately acknowledge the insured about the receipt of claim, provide them with the motor insurance claim form and solicit necessary documents as follows (the list is not exhaustive).

Claim form should be duly completed with the details of the accident and signed by the authorized driver or the insured or their legal representative. Claim form should be submitted along with following general requirements.

Let us have a look into the general requirements and special requirements for processing the claims.

General requirements for motor insurance claims

The following are the general requirements in case of motor insurance claim.

- Original accident report issued by the traffic department

- Original sketch of the accident

- Copy of the insurance policy

- Copy of a valid driving license

- Copy of vehicle registration

- Traffic police reports

- Fire brigade report, where necessary

- Original repair permit issued by traffic department

Special requirements for commercial vehicles

Apart from the general requirements there may special requirements for commercial vehicles as follows,

- Permit

- Fitness certificate

- Any other documents related to usage of the vehicle

Special requirements for third party liability claims

As we have seen earlier that the third party liability claims settlement further can be classified into two types as death or bodily injury and property damage claims.

Third party claims consume a major portion of time of the claims staff. It arises due to the fault of the vehicle insured or its driver. It has to be handled properly to avoid the leakages. The insurance company should be careful when handling the third party insurance claims, as in most of the insurance markets it is a compulsory or mandatory insurance. In some countries the claim settlement is faster, whereas in some countries it may take years before a third party claim is settled. Usually the documents required under third party insurance claim is the court verdict and in case of death of the victim the death certificate along with the postmortem certificate becomes a requirement. The court has to give the verdict against the insured. Based on the verdict the claim is settled. In some countries the death, large bodily injury and large property claims only require courts verdicts. Whereas the smaller claims are settled by the insurance company based on their investigation. If the third party property damage claim is settled without court verdict then the procedure will be similar to own damage claims as mentioned below.

Special requirements for own damage claims

In case of own damage claims, apart from the general requirements, the additional requirement may be the submission of three claims estimates or estimate from the insurance company nominated workshop. Some companies may appoint a third party motor claims loss adjuster, who will assess the claim and submit his report to the insurance company, based on which the claim is processed. The motor loss adjuster is appointed by the insurance company. In some countries the traffic department appoints an agency to estimate the claims to avoid the disputes and manipulations of the claim amounts. Few claims may warrant the insurance company to appoint an investigator to investigate the claim. The role of the investigator is to find the validity of the claim and find the element of fraud if any.

Special requirements for Miscellaneous claims

Other than the own damage claims there are other claims like personal accident claims and workmen compensation claims for the driver and other employees of the insured. In case of death of the covered person apart from the general requirements a death certificate and post mortem certificate may be required. In case of bodily injury, an authorized medical report should be submitted along with the cost of treatment. In case of claim under the workmen compensation extension then the employment certificate will also be required, the workmen compensation cover a wide range of liabilities including the liabilities arising out of death.

Claim registration

The insurance company will register the claim. During the process of claims registration a claim reference number is allotted and it is used as an identity for the claim. A docket is prepared and the provision is made for the claim amount based on the estimate provided or evaluated. The claim docket will contain all the information related to the claim such as policy number, period of insurance, insured name, registration number of the vehicle, date of intimation, date of accident, driver, third party claimants, loss reserve is allocated based on the estimated amount claimed, legal fees and even the name of the legal advisor. All the papers pertaining to the claim are filed in the docket. Normally at the time of registration a close estimate of the claim is taken so as not to have a major deviation at the final assessment and settlement of the claim. The claim estimate is used to make a provision under the claims.

Building rapport with the customer

One of the functions of the claims department is to build the relationship with the customer. The claims department representative will contact the insured and try to guide him in completing the formalities related to the claim lodged. The claims representative may invite the insured to the office for a meeting or may visit the insured to formalize the claim and seek the necessary requirements. The claims representative should understand that the insured has suffered a loss and not in a good state of mind and should express the feeling of empathy whilst dealing with the claimant.

Claims assessment and investigations

Once the claims representative is able to establish the relationship with the claimant. His next job is to make the assessment of the claim. He will try to find the cause of loss and the quantum of loss based on the claims form submitted, estimates received from the garages. He will also look into the police reports, examine the witness and also may cross examine the insured. Where necessary the claims representative may appoint an investigator. The investigator will try to solve the issues related to the suspicious nature of the claim. In some countries there are third party surveyors, appointed by the insurers, who will visit the insured and suggest the names of the workshops where it can be repaired. The assessment job can also be done directly by the skilled claims representative. Once the damaged vehicle is shifted to the workshop, the realistic estimate is worked out. Once the claims representative is satisfied with the cause of loss and the estimate for repairing the vehicle then he will give instruction to repair the vehicle. In third party claims the insurance company will appoint its lawyers in-order to defend its insured if necessary.

Settlement Options

The following options are available for the insurance companies to make the settlement of the claim.

- Repair option

- Reimbursement option

- Replacement option

Repair option

Most of the own damage partial loss claims are settled under this option. Whenever a vehicle is damaged the insurance company will ask the insured either to repair the vehicle in its owned workshop or at a workshop approved by it. In such situation the insured need not pay up front to the workshop. The insured will only pay the deductible and the items which are not covered under the policy. The amount admissible under the policy will be directly settled by the insurance company to the respective workshop.

Reimbursement option

In this type of claim the insured is authorized to repair his vehicle at the workshop of his choice and pay the amount directly to the workshop. The payment amount is assessed and approved by the insurance company in advance. After payment to the workshop the insured will approach the insurance company to recover his claim. He will be asked to submit the original estimate and invoices. Once all the necessary documents are received the claim is settled as agreed and as per the terms of the policy. This option is known as reimbursement option. This is also known as payment option. Almost all third party liability claims, total loss claims and some of the partial losses claims are routed through this option.

Replacement option

This is usually applied in case of total loss claims. When the vehicle is totaled the insurance company has two options either the replace or to make a payment option. If the insurance company chooses the replacement option, they are supposed to provide the insured the same make and model vehicle in lieu of totaled vehicle. However this option is rarely exercised in motor insurance.

Final Settlement of the claim

Once the entire claim settlement process is complete, the claim needs to be settled as soon as possible. Most of the regulators around the world have prescribed time within which the claims has to be settled. The insured should be informed immediately if his claims is denied. In case his claim is admissible and once all the relevant papers are received then the claim should be settled. Any portion of claim which is not payable should be identified and the same should be informed to the claimant. In case of any dispute proper negotiation procedure as outlined in the policy should be followed. If the negotiation is not successful then the insured should be informed about his rights of approaching the regulatory bodies. On handing over the payment and receiving the satisfaction voucher the claims process may not end at the insurer side. However for the insured the process might have ended.

Post claim settlement process

The post claim settlement process can be categorized into three as follows,

- Reinsurance Recoveries

- Selling of salvage and adjusting the settlement

- Recoveries from the third parties

Reinsurance recoveries

Where reinsurance is involved the claims department should provide the necessary papers to the department concerned for recovering the losses from the reinsurers. Normally motor insurance portfolio is fully self-insured by most of the insurance companies. However some high valued cars or a high sum insured for third party and catastrophic losses may be covered through reinsurance. The reinsurance recoveries are not difficult only the procedure should be properly followed. In case of involvement of reinsurers the claims department will forward a copy of settlement papers along with the statement of account on monthly or annual basis as the case may be for recovery from the insurance companies.

Selling of salvage and adjusting the settlement

The claim settlement of motor insurance especially related to the own damage and the third party property damage may result in a good amount of salvage for the insurance company. The insurance company has an option to settle the claim net of salvage or recover the salvage. In case of net of salvage claim settlement there are no recoveries. However where the settlement is based on the recovery of salvage, the salvage becomes the property of the insurance company. Claims representatives are usually tasked with the responsibility of disposal of the salvage. The money recovered in the sale of salvage reduces the claims cost. There are guidelines issued by the insurance companies as the disposal of the salvage.

Recoveries from the third parties

In motor insurance recovery from the third parties play an important role in reducing the claims cost of the insured and the insurance company. If an accident occurs due the fault of the third party the insured and insurance company on behalf of the insured has a right to claim from the third party for the loss which resulted from the accident.

The insurance company will take a subrogation letter from the insured this will give the insurance company right to pursue the recovery from the third parties and this recovery is adjusted in the claim amount thereby reducing the claims cost to the insurance company and the insured. Some companies have a separate recoveries department and in some companies the task is assigned to the claims department. There are third parties involved in the recovery process and if the insurance company decides to outsource the recovery then they can use the services of these third parties. They by their professional capacity are in a better position to recover third party claims then the insurer themselves.

7. <u>Motor surveyors or loss adjusters</u>

Motor Insurance has given rise to a new breed of professionals, who are known as motor claims loss adjusters or also known as surveyors. The loss adjusters can be an independent individual or an organization doing the job of motor loss adjusting. Many accident management companies also do the job of motor loss adjusting or assessing. Most of the Insurance companies have in-house loss adjusting team, which is involved in the processing of the claims with certain limitations. These teams are usually involved in small claims. Whereas in case of large claims or complex claims or claims related to the commercial vehicles are handled by the independent motor loss adjusters.

If the individuals are handling the loss adjusting function then they are supposed to have the minimum mandatory qualification and a license to work as loss adjusters. The organizations should also have a license to operate as a loss adjuster for motor claims. The regulators prescribe the minimum requirements like qualification, fees and mandatory requirements to get the license to act as a motor loss adjuster.

Some of the major functions of the loss adjusters are as follows,

- Pre-risk surveys - Surveying special vehicles

- Spot surveys

- Loss adjusting

- Vehicle valuation

- Fraud investigations

- Disputes handling

Pre-risk surveys

Pre-risk survey is also known as pre-acceptance risk survey. For most types of auto insurance pre-risk inspection is one of the requirement of the underwriters. Before accepting the risk the underwriter wants to be aware of the risk he is accepting. Hence pre-risk surveys help him in assessing the risk. Most of the pre-risk surveys related to motor insurance is usually done by the in-house staff. However in case of specialist risk the survey will be done by the third party surveyors and a professional report is provided by the surveyor. The surveyors usually provide with the photographs of the risk to be insured and they will also provide with the engine number and chassis number of the vehicle. The surveyor also will provide a copy of the registration certificate. They will also comment on the overall condition of the auto along with their recommendation of the valuation.

Spot surveys

Spot surveys are required when there is a major accident, accident to commercial vehicle and accidents involving deaths to the third parties. Some insurance companies have made it mandatory requirement to have spot survey for certain types of claims like commercial vehicle accidents. The spot survey is done at the spot of accident and the surveyor usually takes the pictures of the accident and advices the insured on the process of claim. He also provides a tentative estimate of the loss due to accident, he may also comment on expected hidden damages of the vehicle. They surveyor also gets an opportunity to talk to the witnesses and other parties involved in the accident.

The purpose of spot survey is to help in fraud control.

Loss adjusting

The loss adjusting is one of the important functions of the claims department. Whether it is done in-house or outsourced the following are the important responsibilities of the loss adjuster.

- Primary investigation of the claims filed.

- Confirming the coverage by going through the policy coverage thoroughly.

- Building contact with the insured or the claimant. Also interviewing the other parties related to the claim including the witnesses, mechanics, police and medical personnel etc.

- Inspection of the damaged properties and bodily injuries and or death of the persons.

- Evaluation of the damages or losses relevant to the event.

- Evaluating the various documents related to the claim and meeting the concerned parties where necessary.

- Preparation of the preliminary and final reports of the claim assessment for the insurance companies.

Vehicle valuation

Usually valuation of the auto is required at the time of pre-risk survey and also at the time of accident. However in certain cases the vehicle valuation is done in isolation and is not related to the pre-risk survey or adjusting. In this case the surveyor sees the vehicle and gives his best estimate of the vehicle before insuring the vehicle so that it will aid the insured and the insurer in arriving at the right value of the auto. The surveyor is also involved in assessing the salvage value of the vehicle post-accident so that a correct settlement of the claim is done.

Fraud investigations

It is estimated that there is between 5% - 20% fraudulent claims in motor insurance. In order to avoid these types of claims the insurance companies will engage the services of detectives or investigators. Sometime this role is also performed by the loss adjusting firms or individuals. The investigators role is very comprehensive. He has to visit the scene of accident and find the facts related to the accident. He has to find out the liability in case of liability claims. A thorough research has to done as to the type of coverage and its relationship to the accident. He has to find whether the vehicle was used as per the terms of the policy and whether the driver was qualified to drive the vehicle. Sometime the date of accident is before the inception of the cover. In all such cases the job of the investigator is crucial and he has to get the necessary evidence supported by documents and photographs. Once the investigation is done then the investigator will submit his report. Based on the report of the investigator the insurance company will decide status of the claim. In case of repudiation of the claim the report and contest by the insured the report may become a part of scrutiny by the judicial authority.

Disputes handling

Loss adjusters are the major component of the claims handling process. Hence they not only investigate the claims in case of dispute but also involved in the various dispute resolution methodologies. They may be asked to attend the court proceedings or other mediation methods. Hence the loss adjusters should be familiar with the legal guidelines and processes.

8. <u>Fraud in motor insurance</u>

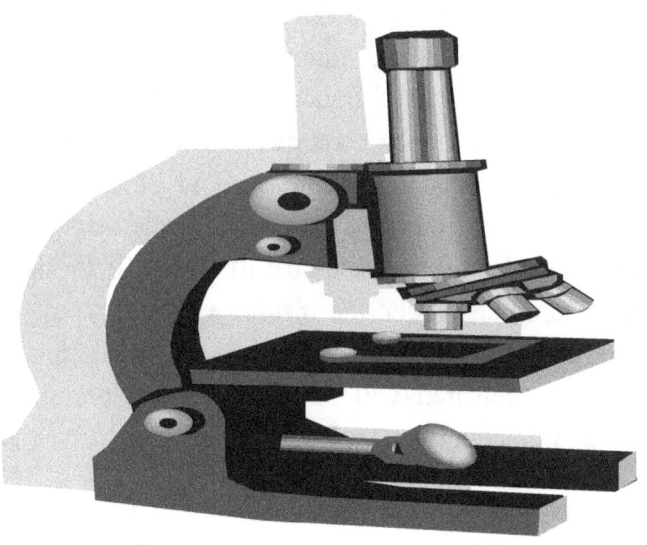

"Fraud is nothing but dishonesty or deception, which is done deliberately with a purpose to benefit or gain". Fraud is considered unethical, illegal and immoral. Fraud is considered as a civil as well as criminal wrong and is punishable by the law. As we all know that the financial industry is prone to the fraud. Insurance industry, which is a part of the financial industry, is the fertile ground for the perpetrators of fraud.

Motor insurance is one of the largest portfolios of business of any country. Hence the chances of fraud are more in the motor insurance sector. There are many parties involved in the motor insurance such as insurers, insured, employers, loss adjusters, hospitals, garages, agencies, lawyers, third parties etc. The involvement of so many parties in the motor insurance process gives scope for perpetrating fraud.

Federal Bureau of Investigation estimates the non-health care fraud at an estimated $40 billion a year. Almost all the insurance companies and countries have experienced one kind or another kind of fraud. The average estimate of fraud in an insurance company dealing with motor insurance may range from 5% to about 20% of the total claim amount. If the fraud is not controlled the innocent insured will have to bear the cost of fraud. If the fraud is plugged completely then the insured cost will come down and the insured may also get the benefit of savings in the claims. The insured will be paying fewer premiums to have the same cover.

Insurers treat fraud as a very serious matter and if at any point of time the insurers are able to get the proof that the insured has indulged in fraud then they have a right to make the contract voidable. Even if it is discovered that the employees of the insurer are involved in the fraud then the insurance company will take a very stern action against their employees.

There are different varieties of frauds.

Based on the party committing the fraud, fraud can be classified as follows,

1. **Insured fraud** - Insured may provide wrong information at the time of taking the policy, which will be difficult to detect. The insured may insure his vehicle giving wrong information about the usage of the vehicle. The vehicle may be used for commercial purposes but for the insurance purpose the insured may declare that the vehicle is being used for private purpose. This will give him a lower rate thereby causing a loss to the insurance company. In case of information related to the driver, wrong information may be given to get a good rate. On the claims side the insured with the collision of garage, lawyers, hospitals, police may lodge fictitious claims and benefit from the insurance policy.

2. **Garage fraud** – The Garages also will be responsible for committing the fraud. They may do so by inflating the bills of labor and parts, they may be billing for the parts, which are purchased but not fixed to the vehicle. They may also buy new original parts and replace the same with duplicate or

second hand parts. The duplicate parts are fraction of the cost compared the cost of the original parts.

3. **Insurance company employee's fraud** – Insurance company employees may become a party to the fraud by co-operating with the fraudsters. They may be aware of the fraud but ignore the signs and symptoms of fraud to get the benefit out of it. They will not follow the check and controls laid down by the organization. Insurance companies treat fraud committed by its employees very seriously and may sack the employee if they get the proof of their involvement. Despite this the employees get involved in committing fraud to get easy money.

4. **Agents and brokers fraud** - The agents and brokers are also known as the intermediaries. They are having the knowledge about the insurance companies and the insurance products. They, because of their knowledge and expertise are capable of committing fraud. They may in their earnestness to help their insured, may get unwittingly involved in committing fraud. There are also cases, where they have committed fraud to get easy money for themselves and their insured.

5. **Other stakeholders fraud** - There are other stakeholders involved in the processing of motor insurance claims and they may also commit fraud like the unscrupulous agents (independent claims

settling agents), by manipulating every aspect of the claims process. Their mission is to work for the customer and to make his non-admissible claim become admissible. They may collude with other partners and succeed in committing fraud against the insurance companies.

6. **Integrated fraud** - In some cases the experienced fraudsters form gangs and involve the insurance company employees, garages, insured, motor loss adjusters and healthcare service providers to commit fraud. This type of fraud is deliberate and difficult to detect and will cost more to the insurance companies.

Based on the types, fraud can be categorized into the following,

1. **Billing for the parts not provided** - This usually happens at the garage. The estimate is made as per the damages to the vehicles and the vehicle is repaired. The bills are provided for the parts needing replacement but on scrutiny it will be found that the part was not provided and the existing part was repaired which would have caused a small labor cost. There will be a huge difference between the labor cost and the cost of replacing the part with the original part. This type of fraud is difficult to detect as the people who are processing the claim may not have any clue as to repairs done to the vehicle. On paper the claim may look great for settlement.

2. **<u>Wrong billing</u>** - This type of fraud occurs when the part replaced is duplicate or second hand and the bill provided is for the original new part. The new part is either returned or used for some other vehicle. The claim processors should be extremely cautious as this type of fraud needs special skills to detect, but may be physically difficult for the claims handler.

3. **<u>Non- disclosure/concealment</u>**- The insured might had an accident and the damages are not visible but hidden. The vehicle is insured as if it were in perfect condition with no accident. Once the policy is issued the insured will lodge a claim, which will be difficult to deny and the insurance company will end up paying the claim, which otherwise is not covered under the policy. Again a person who is experienced or guided by an experienced person will be successful in perpetrating fraud on the insurance company. Whereas there are chances that the timer may be caught in the act. This is not necessarily related to the hidden damages, there are cases when the fraudsters were able to get a claim for the total loss of the vehicle (which was damaged prior to taking of the policy), but the insurance company could not deny the claim because of lack of evidence.

4. **Providing forged bills** – This type of fraud is committed by the insured or with the organized gangs. This type is usually done on reimbursement claims or for international coverage's. The Garage bills are forged and the claim will look like perfect on paper but in reality, the papers are forged and difficult to detect. A thorough investigation will help in catching this type of fraudsters.

5. **Over- billing** - Sometimes the garages will be over billing the insured, when it comes to know that insurance is involved to make the easy extra money from the insurance company. Even the garages approved by the insurance companies may be over-billing the insurance companies for various reasons, sometimes the claims staff may be aware of this type of fraud. It needs strong willed management and less corrupt claims handlers to overcome this type of fraud.

6. **Accident manipulation** – This type of fraud is done by the skilled gangs or individuals in collusion with other stakeholders. The intention is to make the claim amount or money from the insurance company. Sometimes the insured also becomes a party to this type of manipulation and he is also paid a portion of the extra money received through the dishonest act. There are various types of manipulations like stage managed accidents, fake injury claims and forced rear ending.

145

7. **Other types of fraud** – There are many other types of frauds which need to be identified and addressed appropriately. Some of the major one's are non-existent crash of the vehicle, garage for billing purpose only and not for repairs and faking of whip lash and other injuries etc.

Some of the fraud indicators in motor insurance

There is a popular saying that "A person is innocent unless proven guilty". Fraud is also difficult to detect and prove. But there are certain indicators which may help in identifying the Fraud. The indicators are as follows,

1. Perfect documentation is provided by the insured in case of reimbursements.
2. Provision of bills related to expensive parts and inflated labor charges.
3. Insured makes regular accidents and there is a similar billing pattern.
4. The insured provides incorrect contact information on the documents.
5. Variation between the loss estimate and the actual billing on the positive side.
6. The garages showing excessive eagerness whilst processing the claim and for the settlement of the same.

Controlling fraud

Most of the insurers throughout the world are engaged in controlling the fraud. Here are some of the important steps which should help the insurers in controlling the fraud not only in their motor insurance portfolio but also in their overall operations.

1. The insurance companies should have proper internal checks and controls.
2. There should have zero tolerance policy towards the employees who are involved in the fraud.
3. Insurance companies should educate all the stakeholders on the ill effects of fraud.
4. They should have a dedicated email and helpline open for anyone to inform them about the fraud, a sort of whistle blowing policy and the CEO should be directly involved in the investigations of fraud cases brought to their notice.
5. Timely investigation of the cases will help resolve the issues. Any delay in the investigation will jeopardize the results.
6. Post repair survey for vehicles, where expensive parts are replaced will also help in controlling the fraud.
7. Utilization of IT technology, nowadays there are many software's and programs that help in giving an indication of the fraud. They have to be utilized properly to identify the indications of fraud and further investigations.

8. The insurance company should adopt a proactive approach to its underwriting and claims processes.
9. Random auditing and investigation of the claims will help in identifying most of the fraud cases.
10. Involvement of the top management in framing the fraud management policy will make co-operation of all those involved in it a bit easier.
11. An integrated approach should be adopted to address the issue of fraud by having a regular involvement of the insured, loss adjuster, garages and other service providers.

9. <u>Reinsurance of motor insurance portfolio</u>

Reinsurance is the terminology with which most of insurers are familiar but general public may not be so well aware of. If we look at it plainly it is similar to insurance which an ordinary layman purchases. The only difference is that reinsurance is available to the insurance companies and not to the ordinary customers. In insurance the insured is the person who needs protection and he buys protection by way of the insurance. Whereas the insurance companies who deal in different kinds of risks also need to protect themselves hence they have to buy insurance to protect them-selves. Reinsurance is nothing but the "insurance for the insurers".

Reinsurance is very vital to the insurance industry. The globalization and the internet revolution has made the reinsurance transactions much easier and helped the reinsurers in mapping their risks in-order to avoid accumulations. Almost all of the insurance markets in the world are regulated. This has resulted in increasing compliances with the regulators and their requirements.

The insured is not a party to the re-insurance contract; the reinsurance contract is between the insurance company and the reinsurer. Let us look briefly into the forms and types of reinsurances.

There are two basic forms of reinsurance as below,

- Facultative reinsurance
- Treaty reinsurance

Facultative reinsurance

Facultative reinsurance is also known as case by case insurance or optional insurance. Facultative is a French word and was coined in the early 19th century, its meaning was occurring optionally. It is the oldest form of reinsurance. In this type of the reinsurance, the reinsurers have an option to accept or decline risks which are offered to them, even the insurer also have a right to place or not to place a risk. The insurer negotiates with the each reinsurer separately and each risk is evaluated individually. It is time consuming process and does not guarantee placement of the risk.

Treaty insurance

Treaty insurance is also known as obligatory reinsurance and automatic insurance. Under treaty reinsurance the reinsurer is obliged to accept cessions within the terms and conditions of the agreement and the insurer are obliged to cede the risk. Under treaty the reinsurer cannot refuse to accept the risk which are within the scope of the agreement, however they have every right to deny any risk which is outside the scope of the treaty. Initially the concept of reinsurance started with the facultative insurance but as the complexity increased, treaty became a more popular form of reinsurance.

There are two types of reinsurance as follows,

- Proportional reinsurance
- Non-proportional reinsurance

Proportional reinsurance

Proportional reinsurance means reinsurers take an agreed or stated percent share of each policy that insurance company writes. The premiums, risks and the claims are shared in equal proportions. Proportional reinsurance is usually done under the following heads,

> ➤ Facultative
> ➤ Facultative obligatory
> ➤ Quota share treaty
> ➤ Surplus treaty
> ➤ Open cover and pools

Non-proportional reinsurance

In Non-proportional reinsurance the premiums and loss (claims are not shared in proportion). Usually in these type of contracts the liability between the insurance company and the reinsurer is focused on the basis of loss occurring.

Non-Proportional reinsurance is divided into the following types,

> ➤ Excess of loss
> ➤ Stop loss

Arranging reinsurance program

Motor insurance is an attrition class of business. The claims under motor are of three types, own damage claims, third party claims and miscellaneous claims. Under these claims we find smaller claims which are of high frequency and the large claims, which are of low frequency. The severity of low frequency claims are high. Frequency refers to the number of time the claim is occurring. The severity refers to the very high value of the claims arising out of single event. The insurance companies would want to go in for self-insurance of most of the motor risks. High value cars are usually reinsured, the overall portfolio may also be reinsured to protect against a combination of losses including the catastrophic losses.

Most of the insurance companies have to struggle with their Motor insurance portfolios. The best way to overcome this struggle with the portfolio is to have a robust underwriting and claims system in place; apart from it they should also make sure that they have a right re-insurance program in place. To have a right reinsurance program the following basic steps need to be followed.

- ✓ Identify and analyze the basics for reinsurance
- ✓ Selecting the right reinsurance program
- ✓ Placement of the reinsurance program
- ✓ Reviewing the reinsurance program

Identify and analyze the basics for reinsurance

Before getting into any reinsurance arrangement, it is better that both the parties to the Re-insurance contract have a proper understanding of the arrangement of the risk transfer. The insurer should understand the exact form of reinsurance required and other parameters like retention, coverage and the limits of reinsurance required.

The insurance company should be able to analyze and identify the exposures to its portfolios by the size and type of risks. The exposure can be due acute cases, major unforeseen accumulations and high sum insured. Once it identifies the exposures then it can fix its retentions.

Retentions are decided based on many factors. The main purpose is to have an underwriting stability. The insurance company is the custodian of funds belonging to the insured's, the insurance company should see to it that the money is adequately protected against loss. Reinsurance is one of the best way of protecting the portfolio from major loss exposures.

Selecting the right reinsurance program

Once the retention levels are decided then the insurance company has to select the right type of reinsurance program and the right reinsurers.

There are various types of reinsurers and reinsurance programs. The insurance companies based upon their financial analysis and technical analysis will be in a position to take a decision as to the suitable type of reinsurance. As far as motor insurance is concerned the treaty is the right type of route and under treaty the insurers should be able to decide the suitability of the program. As the loss ratios under motor insurance normally crosses 40% and sometimes it goes beyond 130%, which may be a big cause of concern to the insurers as the volume of business is high so naturally the losses will also be high. Hence as far as motor insurance is concerned a non-proportional reinsurance will help in protecting the insurance companies from losses beyond a certain limit. In case of proportional reinsurance the losses are shared for each and every claim and this will help in reducing the portion of liability of the insurer.

Placement of the reinsurance program

After identifying and analyzing the reinsurance requirements and selection of reinsurance program the next step is the placement of the reinsurance program. The insurance company has to decide in which market it is better to place the risk and whether it should be either direct or through a broker. In some markets a broker has to be involved for placement whereas in some markets direct placement can be done. A vast majority of reinsurers are from the countries which has a strong regulatory control and these companies are financially very sound and with a very high credit rating. Hence placing the business directly with these companies is not only secure but also prestigious. It again depends upon the insurance company which is placing the business if the insurance company is reputed then it will not be difficult for it to find a good re-insurer. But if the insurance company is a new company, then it will be easier for it to approach a broker to get the right coverage. Broker by virtue of their experience, market knowledge and relationship with the reinsurers will be able to place the business in the international market. They will also be in a position to administer the business to the satisfaction of both the insurers and the reinsurer.

The insurance company is interested to protect it selves from the catastrophic losses and accumulated losses in the motor portfolio. Usually a combination of self-insurance and the non-proportional insurance will help in protecting the portfolio. Some companies also use the proportional form of reinsurance to protect their portfolio. High value

155

cars are usually fully reinsured under treaty or facultative reinsurance.

Reviewing the reinsurance program

The best reinsurance program also has to be reviewed as we are living in a dynamic environment. Each day changes are occurring, which are in the form of new risks, currency fluctuations, wars, economic recession, bankruptcies, Tsunami, etc., The Review should be a continuous process and it should begin well ahead of time of placement or renewal.

10. <u>Consumer protection</u>

The purpose of insurance is to provide the necessary financial compensation at the time of claim. The insurance is nothing but a promise to pay in case of insured loss. The promise may be in the form of a document which may cost the insurers on an average anywhere between US $ 10 to

US$ 100. But in terms of collection, the insurers may be collecting the premiums anywhere from US $100 to more than US$ 10,000,000.

Insurers are the custodians of the premiums collected from the insured hence they have to make sure that funds collected from the insured are not misused and they are available at the time of settlement of the claim. The contract wording are framed by the insurer hence the contract of agreement is known as contract of adhesion, in which case one party to the contract i.e., the customer or the insured has to adhere to the contract prepared by the insurance company . In such situations there are chances that the wording may be prepared to harm the interests of the insured.

In order to protect the interest of the insurers there are various governmental systems in place. The three major systems which help the customer to safeguard their interest and to make the insurers responsible are as follows,

- Regulatory authority

- Consumer courts

- Other legal systems - courts

Regulatory authority

Almost all the countries in the world have thriving insurance industry. The Governments will appoint a regulator to control the insurance industry. The main purpose of the regulator is to protect the customers or the consumers. The customer, who purchases the insurance coverage, is also known as the insured. He is usually at the receiving end as the terms and conditions are framed by the insurance companies and he is merely forced to accept them and adhere to them. In order to protect the customer the insurance company should have the credit worthiness to pay the claims. The insurance companies are the custodians of the funds belonging to the policyholders and shareholders. It is imperative that these funds are invested safely, the regulator will frame the rules for the investment of the money generated by the insurers. Moving backwards for the protection of the customer it is also important to make sure that the insurance company is also protected, this will indirectly protect the rights of the the owners. The regulator also gets involved in the development and setting of the professional standards for the insurance industry.

The regulators have their mission statement or purpose of their coming into being. The mission statement incorporates the following items and these are not the only items it may vary depending upon the local requirements and conditions.

- Protecting the policy holders.
- Protecting the shareholders.
- Fair treatment of the policy holders.
- Promoting the ethical and professional standards of the industry.
- Toning up the claim settlement procedures.
- Provision of the disputes redressal mechanism.

- Building systems to maintain the minimum level of solvency margins.
- Assisting with the compulsory insurances.
- Setting the qualification standards of the employees.

Let us now have a look into some of the duties and responsibilities of the insurance regulator,

- Regulating, controlling, registering and licensing the insurance companies and the insurance service providers.
- Protecting the interests of the policy holders.
- Promoting efficiency and fair trade practices in the industry.
- Controlling and regulating all the aspects of the insurance industry including the product approvals.
- One of the major areas handled by the regulators is addressing of the disputes between the parties to the insurance contract and the ancillary players.
- Regulation and controlling the solvency margin, investment of funds, re-insurance placement and other financial functions.
- Regulating and controlling the funds for social causes.
- Development of the professionalism in the insurance industry, through minimum educational requirements.
- Formulating and implementation of the code of conduct standards for the Industry.

In India the insurance regulator is the Insurance Regulatory and Development Authority also known as IRDA, one of their primary missions to is to protect the interest of and secure fair treatment of policy holders. In Saudi Arabia the insurance regulatory role is performed by the Saudi Arabian Monetary Agency (SAMA), which was initially formed to regulate the banking sector. In United Kingdom the insurance industry is regulated by the Financial Conduct Authority (FCA). Each country may have its own regulatory authority.

The regulatory authorities have very standard mechanism of addressal of the consumer disputes. The regulators basically prescribe minimum mandatory requirements to be complied by the insurance companies in terms of disputes handling. The policy document should contain the mechanism of handling of the dispute related to the insurance. There are time-lines prescribed by the regulators for the handling of the claims, complaints and disputes. The insurance companies should have proper checks and controls along with the systems and procedures for the compliance of the regulatory requirements. However in case the customer is not satisfied with the settlement then he has to be informed about the procedure of approaching the regulator so that his grievances are addressed properly.

The regulator usually forms a committee or a body within the regulators office, which will look into the complaints from the policy holders. Their job is to make sure that the justice is done and the confidence of the policy holders is maintained or reinforced. The presence of regulator has made it easy for the policy holders to lodge a complaint against erring insurance providers. The regulatory body by virtue of their knowledge and expertise are able to see through the game of the insurance companies and are able to reprimand the erring insurers (where necessary), so that the policy holder is not made to suffer. The disputes redressal body should also take care of the insurer also and make sure that the insurers do not become prey to the unreasonable demands of the policy holders. Moreover they do not get into financial mess for the sake of business and investment.

There are certain pre-conditions which have to be met before the policy holder can approach the redressal body. The first pre-condition may be that they have to first lodge the complaint with the insurance provider and there is time limit within which the insured should approach the regulatory authority after rejection of his complaint or non-response to his complaint.

The redressal body may be called by different names like insurance ombudsman, disputes redressal committee, complaint redressal forum, disputes conciliation board or simply consumer protection department. The main purpose of the body is to make sure that they help in receiving the complaints from the policy holders against the insurer. The disputes may relate to the policy wording, delay and non-delivery of documentation, non-renewal, denial of coverage, claim settlement problems. The complaint process is simple and usually free. The body will give award which is binding on the insurance company. However if the customer is not satisfied with the award he can approach the Consumer Courts or the other legal systems of the country.

Consumer courts

Consumer courts are one of the most important bodies, which is responsible for the protection of the consumer rights. The consumer courts are accessible to the buyers of all kinds of goods including the insurance. Insurance is coming under the service industry and it fulfills the needs of the customer by selling insurance policies. Hence the buyers of the insurance policy are also considered as the consumer as per their definition of the consumer courts. The insured can approach the consumer court located in his jurisdiction.

The consumer courts may be categorized depending upon the geographical coverage it will provide to the consumers. Then they may also have the monetary ceiling limits for the cases they are supposed to handle. Hence in case of large claims the consumer has to approach a higher level court and for smaller to medium claims he can approach the lower court. The courts can be categorized based on their presence in the individual districts, states and the country.

The procedure of most the consumer courts are very simple and a complaint can be lodged by the consumer. An average consumer with basic understanding of the financial and legal system does not need any help of any agents or experts. However if the consumer would like to hire the services of the legal expert then they can hire them on fee basis or no fee no cure basis. The fees based legal expert may charge a nominal fee but the no fee no cure basis expert may charge a big percentage of the amount recovered from the seller. The percentage may range anywhere between 5% - 25%. These experts have knowledge and experience and they help the consumer in pursuing their claims against the seller.

Some consumer courts even provide free legal aid to the consumer, if he is unable to afford a legal expert. As far as the fee is concerned, there is no fee for lodging a complaint in the consumer court. However in certain countries a nominal fee is charged and which is refundable if the consumer wins the case.

The consumer courts can also be of 2 tier system or more than two tier system and in case the consumer is not satisfied he can approach a higher court and appeal against the order. One of the important aspects of the filing of the first complaint and subsequent appeal is that it has a time limit. Hence if there is a delay in filing the case then the case will become "time barred". A "time barred" claim is not admissible in the court. The limitation of the time may be anywhere between 30 days to 365 days. The consumer has to follow the procedures laid down by the consumer courts. The documentation is insisted upon in the local language or national language and if the documentation is in any other language then it has to be translated in the local language.

Unlike in the past the consumer courts nowadays are more active and are able to dispose the cases at a much faster pace. Most of the consumers feel satisfied after going through the procedures of the consumer courts.

Other legal systems - Courts

In case of consumer disputes related to motor insurance, it is always recommended to approach a consumer court rather than the civil court.

However every country has their own legal systems and the legal systems operate under common law and will cover various facets of human life. If the consumer or the insured is not satisfied with the consumer court or he may wish not to approach the consumer court and directly go the court under common law, he may do so. Even the courts work in 2 tier or more than 2 tier system. If the lower court awards a judgment in favor of the consumer then the seller can appeal against the judgment in the next level of the court and this may go on till the court in the final tier. The insurer by virtue of his money and offices across the country will be able to easily sustain the time and cost needed for the case. But going to the court, may take time and will need expertize as far as insured is concerned. In such situation he has to hire the services of the legal expert or an advocate. The legal expert will file a case on behalf of the consumer and normally he charges fees for his services. There is no guarantee that the consumer will win the case against the seller. The cases in the court may drag on for years, thereby exhausting the consumer both in terms of time and money.

In some countries there are small claims courts or disputes tribunals. They may have their judicial function limited to an amount prescribed for them and they will not take cases which are beyond the monetary limits.

Motor insurance is one of the portfolios, causing a huge number of disputes. The disputes may be related mostly to the claims section rather than the underwriting part. To address the claims issues some countries like India have a separate body which addressed the issues related to the motor vehicle accidents. The name of the body is Motor Accident Claims Tribunal (MACT) and it is formed under the Motor Vehicle Act of India.

12. <u>Information technology and the motor insurance</u>

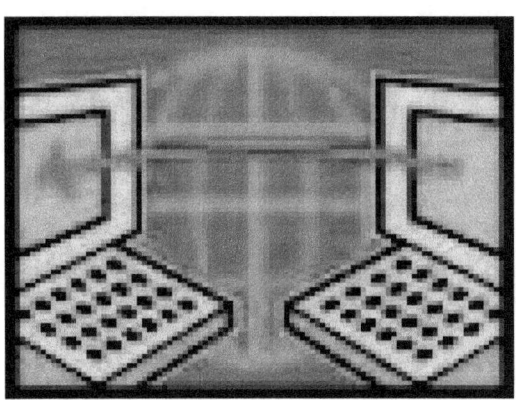

The information technology is vital and has become an integral part of the insurance industry. The insurance industry deal with a large volume of data and it has to be used in the right way to get the synergy of the operations. The insurance industry is facing the real challenges of risk management, rating, claims handling, provision of terms

167

and fraud management etc. They would like to operate more efficiently and expect the real co-operation and co-ordination among the different units within the organization and the outside bodies.

As the insurance penetration is increasing throughout the world there is a greater need for decisions to sustain and grow the business. The decisions have to be taken based on the information available and the information technology plays an important role in providing the quality and type of information needed by the management.

Motor insurance has become one of the major portfolios of insurance companies. It is also the major portfolio of several consumers. Hence it requires a major attention. The regulation in many countries has put a lot of pressure on the motor insurers to provide the covers mandated by the regulators and face the competition from the fellow insurers. The escalating costs of spare parts and labor charges have put the insurers in a dire situation. The information technology has helped in reducing the data handling cost and it has also become a tool for underwriting and handling fraud.

The insurance companies can hire the services of the external IT consultants or they may have their own in-house IT experts who may be able to help in designing the right systems of operations. The insurance companies area always keen to participate in the motor insurance even though it is an attrition class of business. The motor insurance provides a bulk of business and also helps in retaining the customers, who provide composite business. If the management of this class of business is not done properly the insurance company may end up in losses. Most of the countries have made it compulsory for the owners of the vehicle to have third party insurance. Hence it will be impossible for the motor insurers or the composite insurers to stay away from the motor insurance portfolio. They have to learn to manage the portfolio in a more scientific way to make profits from the account.

Information technology can play an important role from the negotiation stage till the expiry of the policy period and it will continue on the renewal.

IT can be used in the following stages of the product life.

- Selling
- Underwriting
- Claims
- Accounts
- Renewals

Selling

IT has come as a boon to selling function. Selling is nothing but converting the service or product into money. Selling is one of the major function of insurance and it starts with planning, prospecting and continues during the policy period and at the time of renewal. During negotiation, it can help the salesman in giving the presentation of the product and storing the information related to the customer, which will help him customer segmentation and mapping of the customer. It will help the salesman in making reminders of the meetings of the customer and sending the information needed by the customer like the coverage details, proposal forms, claim forms, list of network providers, satisfied customers list and also personal greetings as a part of sales process. It also helps in identifying the profitable customers and the productive agents and brokers. It makes the job of the insured and the insurers easier. The insurers have less botheration in preparing and submitting the quotation and renewal reminders. Nowadays it is easier to get online quotes and online renewal or purchasing of the personal lines policy. It is much more simpler to buy an online motor insurance policy, it has helped people save their time and money on insurance.

Underwriting

Underwriting is the process of identifying the risks as insurable and uninsurable and if insurable then providing the necessary terms and conditions for insurance. It heavily relies on information technology in looking at the historical data as well as the actuarial pricing, which in turn uses the information technology in working out the prices. Nowadays there are smart systems and software's which help the underwriting in arriving at the right rate for a risk based on the information and parameters pre-fed into the system. The systems help in providing the risk profile information, policy content, identifying the areas of re-insurance, endorsements and payment terms with reminders etc.

Claims

The insurance company sells a promise to make good the financial loss incurred by the insured due to an insured risk. Hence the processing of the claims is very important. If processing of the claims has to stand the requirements of the regulator and the satisfaction of the customer. The IT will help in the various areas of claims processing like valuation of the risk, receiving the complaints in respect of inadequacy of the claim settlement, claim notification, checking the requirement of policy validity, premium payment etc. Fraud is one of the important areas of claims management; IT will help in identifying the fraud and its indicators. It also helps in predicting the possibility of fraud. Controlling fraud will help in reducing the cost of claims for the insurers. The IT also helps in reinsurance recoveries in a well-organized way.

Accounts

Collection of premium and settlement of claims are two major functions of the insurance company. Apart from this the insurance companies also invest their funds to make sure that they generate income out of the investments. The IT has helped the insurance companies in integrating this functions and providing the tools for better decision making. With IT the job of the Accountant has become easier, he can send the account statements online without going into the printing and posting option as was done in the past.

Renewals

Insurance contracts are for twelve months and the policies need to be renewed every year. IT helps the insurance companies in providing information related to renewal in nut shell and it also assists the insurer to red flag the policies which are not to be renewed. The renewal even though may not be an obligation on part of the insurance company in general sense but it may be a mandatory requirement in some countries. Even from business prudence it is advisable to send the renewal notice to the existing customer's at least few weeks in advance.

Information Sharing

Information sharing is an important area of motor insurance. Now with technology it is easy to share the information related to the insured. In some countries there are independent operators who link the insurance companies enlisted with them for sharing the information related to vehicles and insured. This will greatly help in addressing the fraud cases and dealing with difficult insured. The insurance companies may be asked to pay an annual fee, which will enable them to share the information and access the information required for underwriting and claims purposes.

12. <u>Marketing mix of motor insurance</u>

<u>Insurance Market</u>

There are various definitions for "Market". Our definition of the Insurance Market is a place where the buyers and sellers gather or come together for commercial purpose. It may be a physical market place or a virtual market.

Apart from the buyers and sellers of insurance there are other players who are directly or indirectly involved in the insurance market such as garages, agents, brokers, consultants, advisors, surveyors, loss adjusters, loss assessors, actuaries, regulators, educational institutions, risk managers, banks, reinsurers etc. The main players of the insurance market are the buyers of insurance and the sellers of insurance the buyers are called as insured and the sellers are known as the insurance companies or brokers or agents etc.

In Motor insurance we focus on the insurance companies, insured, re-insurers, brokers, agents, consultants, advisors and risk managers. They all play an important role in the process of sale of an insurance policy.   Whereas the reinsurers do not directly participate in the marketing process but like a supplier they help and protect the insurance company by providing them with the necessary reinsurance   coverage.   Large   customers   will   give importance to the backing of a good reinsurer.

The buyers are also known as the customers of insurance and are usually categorized into mainly two segments, personal lines and commercial lines. The personal lines are composed of individuals who buy insurance for their own self consumption. The commercial lines are composed of individuals, who run businesses and corporate bodies. There may be further categorization of personal lines by identifying different segments like High Net worth Individuals (HNI) and Ultra High Net worth Individuals (UHNI). These segments target the top rich people in the market. In commercial insurance also there may be further classification of the customer based on the Ownership (private and public bodies etc.), size of the organization, region etc.

The sellers of insurance are the insurance companies. The insurance companies are categorized into direct selling insurance companies and in-direct selling insurance companies. The direct selling insurance companies sell their policies directly to the customer. They can do it directly through their sales staff, having an arrangement with franchisees and opening many point of sale offices. They also use the IT technology and internet to increase their sales. The indirect companies sell through intermediaries; the intermediaries can be the agent, broker, consultant, bank or any other individual or juristic entity which will get the business for the insurance company for a fee or commission. Commission is part of premium which is paid to the agent or broker or any other service provider for their services. Some companies may be a mix of direct and indirect companies as they do business directly and also through the intermediaries. Nowadays even intermediaries are using internet to get the customers.

The insurance companies can also be categorized into life insurance companies and general insurance companies. The life insurance companies deal with the life insurance or also known as the protection and savings insurance, whereas the general insurance companies deal with non-life products, some general insurance companies deal with life products also. The general insurance companies can also be further divided into the line of business they are doing like marine insurance company, health insurance company, motor insurance company. These are also known as specialist insurance companies as they deal only in one class of business. The companies which deal with more than one class of business are termed as composite insurance company.

Marketing is an important function of insurance company. Philip Kotler, a well-known authority on marketing has defined marketing as 'Satisfying needs and wants through an exchange process'.

Insured needs protection against financial loss and this need is being satisfied by the insurance company in the form of issuance of insurance policy which guarantees the insured against the financial loss against the insured perils, which is subject to the terms and conditions of the policy. Insurance is a promise to make good a financial loss for a consideration which is termed as premium. In insurance the insurance company offers only a document, which promises to compensate the insurance in case of admit-able loss under the policy. The document (policy) may be worth few dollars and the premium received by the insurance company may be in millions, whereas the claim may be astronomical high.

Insurance is not a tangible product, it is considered as a services product. Hence marketing of motor insurance is like marketing of services. A major portion of marketing of insurance product is selling. Selling is an integral part of marketing process.

There are 7 Ps of services marketing; this is beyond the traditional concept of marketing mix which used to have 4 Ps of marketing. Let us have a brief look into the 7 Ps of marketing mix related services marketing.

1. Product
2. Price
3. Place
4. Promotion
5. People
6. Process
7. Physical Evidence

Product

Motor insurance policy is an intangible, heterogeneous and perishable product. The product can be customized as per the requirement of the customer. One customer may require a small sum insured and another customer may require a larger sum insured. Even within the same product there may be differentiation, let us take for example in case of packaged policy one customer may opt for dealer repair option and another may opt for higher third party liability limits and rent a car option. Some customer may opt for outside jurisdiction coverage. Some would like to have additional personal accident coverage to the driver and the passengers. In motor insurance one of the common aspect is that almost all the countries in the world have a minimum mandatory insurance coverage linked to the motor insurance and this coverage is termed and mandatory third part insurance. Under this type of coverage the mandatory cover wordings are prescribed by the regulator. The insurers have an option to give any add on covers. However the insurer can get the customers based on the reputation, services and rates. The insurance service is also perishable if not utilized.

Pricing

Pricing in simple terms is determining the cost of the services offered, in motor insurance it is the determination of the premium of the product. The actuary will build the basic premium and various factors are added to it like operating costs, marketing costs, reserves, commission offered to the intermediaries and reinsurance costs etc. Then the rates so arrived are again subject to modification depending upon the quality of service being offered by the insurance company, the insured past claims experience and the type of the client. However in insurance price plays an important role in the sale and purchase of the product.

Place

The term place in the marketing refers to the distribution of the product. The motor insurance product can be sold directly by the insurance company through its employed salesman and this type of distribution is known as direct selling. Whereas they can also avail the services of Brokers and Agents to sell their products, such a mode of selling is known as indirect selling. In the direct selling the insurers do not pay any commission to any outside agencies. However in the indirect channel they have to pay the commission to the outside agencies, commonly known as intermediaries. Some marketers of motor insurance follow a mix method they have their own sales team and they also rely on the business through the broker and the insurance agents. In motor insurance the car dealers and the vehicle registration agents also play an important role in selling the insurance as agents. By virtue of their presence in the right location they are able to get the right business at right place. Nowadays we find that the opportunities provided by the internet to the marketers are immense, the motor insurers are also able to exploit this opportunity by selling some of their restricted policies through internet (online marketing).

Promotion

Promotion is communication with the existing and the potential customers about the offering or the brand of the organization. The promotional activities may include advertisements, direct marketing, point of sale (POS) banners, sales promotion and even sponsoring events for the benefit of the society. The purpose of promotion is to persuade the customer to be aware of the brand and the offerings of the company with the ultimate aim to sell the product or services.

People

In the service marketing the people of an organization play an important role in the sale of product. In the product marketing, it is more a product which sells rather than the people, who service the product. Especially marketing motor insurance need people with special skills to market the product. A person with empathy will be a better salesperson than the person who is lacking empathy. The role of the salesman or the sales manager who is interfacing with the customer is important. The people will buy from the person whom they trust and if the sales person is not trustworthy then the chances of his clinching the sales are less. Insurance is an annual contract hence after the expiry of the policy it has to be renewed. Hence there has to be a trustworthy relationship not only in explanation of the product but also in the settlement of the claims. The trustworthiness of the sales person in the relationship will help in continuing the relationship. The attitude of the people dealing with the customers is very important, their treatment of the customer, their addressing the concerns of the customers, their handling of the documentation and their handling of the claims are all of concern from the point of view of the customer. Insurance company may lose a chunk of its business, the moment it loses an excellent salesman. The insurance companies should integrate their services which are behind the sales person so that the person interfacing the customer is able to deliver the impeccable service. In insurance industry, as per the regulations a person selling the motor insurance policies need to have certain minimum technical competency, which is acquired by passing an examination made mandatory by the local regulator. In some countries it is mandatory to undergo minimum number of hours of training and pass an examination to acquire a license to sell the insurance.

Process

Like any service industry motor insurance is also a strong service oriented industry depended on the delivery of its service. The process of delivery is very important in insurance as the person approaches the insurance company in times of distress. The claims handling process has to be streamlined with the proper checks and controls. The responsibilities and accountabilities should be properly fixed. The times for processing of the approvals, settlement of claims, addressal of complaints should be fixed and it should be made sure that they are strictly adhered to. The motor insurance companies should provide a 24 hours helpline to the customers with the purpose of helping the processing of the claims, towing of the vehicle and addressing of their queries related to the insurance and also helps them in addressing the issues related to coverage's and other legal issues. The insurance company can hire the services of the third party provider, who can provide dedicated 24 hour helpline.

Physical Evidence

The physical evidence is the tangible evidence of the insurance company selling motor insurance. It can be the location of the office; the location may be in the prestigious building, which gives a good impression to the customer. It may the designing of the office both interior and exterior. A good design will give a better image of the company. The other evidences may the dressing of the employees of the insurance company, their brochures, business cards, proposal forms, receipts and policy documentation etc.

Glossary of motor insurance terms

Accident: An accident is defined a sudden, fortuitous event or an unexpected, unforeseen event resulting in a loss.

Actual cash value: see market value.

Actuary: Actuary is the person who works on insurance risks and premiums. They are involved in determining the prices of insurance by studying trends and analyzing different parameter. Nowadays they are also involved as a link between the regulator and the insurance company.

Adverse selection: The underwriter is exposed to a higher risk, which is not factored at the time of inception of the coverage.

Agent: An agent is an individual or a juristic person who sells insurance on commission basis and mostly they are exclusive agents. They sell for only one insurance company.

Agreed value: This concept is applicable to the vehicles which are antique pieces or custom made. The sum insured is arrived based on the agreement between the insured and the insurance company. This sum insured forms the basis of contract and in case of total loss the value agreed upon is paid to the insured. The sum insured so agreed is the agreed value.

Amendment: See endorsement.

Blue book: A book available in certain countries which will provide the market values of the automobiles and aids the insurers and the insured to arrive at the right value for insurance.

Bodily injury: An injury sustained by a person.

Cancellation: Termination of an insurance contract before the end of the policy period.

Catastrophe: Extremely unfortunate incident causing enormous damages to the persons and the properties.

Examples of catastrophes are floods, earthquake and hailstorms etc.

Claim: Application for payment under the terms of the insurance policy.

Claim adjuster: In-house or outsourced person responsible for assessment, investigating and processing of a claim.

Claimant: Individual or juristic person presenting a claim.

Clause: Clause is a section in an insurance policy such as depreciation clause and co-insurance clause, the clause gives a detailed explanation related to the additional term to the policy.

Combined Single limit: Under combined single limit the coverage for property damage and the death or bodily injury are clubbed or combined together and as one single amount of coverage.

Commercial lines: The Insurance policies designed for and bought by businesses or juristic persons or individual running businesses.

Commission: It is the part of premium which is paid to the agent or broker or any other service provider for their services.

Conditions: Conditions are the duties and responsibilities the insured and the insurance company.

Contract: It is a legal agreement between two parties.

Damage: Causing harm to the person or the property resulting in financial loss.

Deductible: Portion of insurance claim, which has to be paid by the insured.

Depreciation: Reduction in value of any property due to wear and tear.

Discount: Reduction in the premium cost. It is usually based on complying of certain conditions resulting in good feature or insuring a large number of vehicles with low loss ratios.

Effective date: The date on which the insurance policy begins or becomes effective.

Endorsement: It is a document forming a part of the policy or an additional attachment which amends the policy.

Estimate: It is an approximate cost to repair a damaged vehicle.

Exclusion: An item which is not covered by the insurance policy.

Experience rating: Rating the risk based on the past claims experience of the risk.

Expiry date: The date on which the motor insurance coverage ends.

First party: In insurance contract the insured is referred as the first party.

Fraud: The insurance the insured has to disclose the information and he cannot conceal the information intentionally or unintentionally. Misrepresentation or concealment of the material fact is treated as fraud.

Frequency: The number of times an accident occurs.

Hazard: It is chance of increasing the loss due to a peril.

Hit and run: Hit and run occurs when any vehicle does not stop after an accident.

Inception date: The beginning date of the coverage as mentioned in the insurance policy.

Indemnity: It is one of the important principles of insurance which states that the insured should be in the similar condition after the loss as he was before the loss.

Independent adjuster: Independent adjuster can be an individual or a legal entity, who will estimate the losses occurring due to an accident. He is an outside person and not employed by the insurance company.

Insurable interest: Insurable interest is simply ownership. A person or an entity has an insurable interest if he owns the item or subject matter to be insured. But on a broader front without ownership if a person has financial interest in a particular risk, then also it is considered as an insurable interest.

Liability: Any legally enforceable obligation or responsibility for the injury or damage suffered by another person.

Insured: The person holding the insurance policy is known as insured, they are also referred as assured.

Market value: The fair market value of vehicle, which is the replacement cost less depreciation.

Negligence: Failure to exercise proper care that is expected of a reasonable person.

Null and void: A policy which becomes invalid and will have no legal force.

Peril: Peril is the cause of loss example can be accident, flood and earthquake etc.

Policy period: The period during which the policy is in force.

Pre-accident condition: The condition of the vehicle before the accident.

Proximate cause: It is defined as the cause which leads to a chain of events leading to the loss without the intervention of another event. The proximate cause can be the first cause or last cause or may be the dominant cause.

Red Book: See Blue book. It is similar to blue book.

Reinsurance: Insurance for insurers.

Renewal: The continuation of in-force policy by invitation and payment of necessary premium or agreement.

Salvage: Value derived from the damaged property is known as salvage.

Satisfaction voucher: A form certifying that the insured is satisfied with the vehicle repairs. It is duly signed and delivered by the insured.

Severity: Quantum of the claim arising out of single event.

Split Limit: A split limit or separate limit coverage policy splits the limit of coverage's into property damage coverage and death or bodily injury coverage.

Subrogation: Subrogation is nothing but assuming the legal rights of a person for which the expenses or claim has been paid. It can be termed as substitution, substituting the place of the insured.

Theft: The unlawful taking of another's property with the intent to permanently deprive the owner of its use or possession.

Third party: Any party other than the insurer and the first party, usually having a financial interest in the agreement between the insured and the insurance company.

Third party claim: The third party claims arises when the accident is caused by the fault of the insured driver. It is a claim brought by the third party against the insured driver for financial loss occurring due to motor vehicle accident.

Total Loss: Total loss in motor insurance is considered when the damage of the vehicle is so high that the repair cost will exceed the value of the vehicle.

Underwriting: Underwriting as the process of analyzing the risk, determining the premium, other terms and conditions, monitoring the account post acceptance. The process an insurer goes through to determine whether or not it will provide coverage for an applicant.

ABOUT THE AUTHOR

Mohammed Sadullah Khan, is a Senior Faculty Member at the Course design and delivery section, The Institute of Finance (Saudi Arabian Monetary Agency). He did his M.B.A. (University Topper), Fellow of Insurance Institute of India and Chartered Insurance Practitioner cum Fellow of Chartered Insurance Institute (UK). He has more than 28 years of experience in the Insurance Industry of which almost 21 years in Saudi Arabia.

He worked for Royal and SunAlliance Insurance Company in Riyadh and Dammam, also worked as a (Direct Recruit) for New India Assurance Company at Mumbai. He worked for India's South Central Railways, General Manager for the Landmark Marketing Agencies for their food and Office equipment division. He taught Management subjects to MBA students and guided them in their Market Research Projects as a Faculty Member at IIAS, served as Consulting Director, for CMS, Mumbai, He has also done numerous Research Projects for CMS, NIACL, R & SA and MARG – Market Research Group (currently owned by AC Neilsen).

He was the founder and insurance columnist for insurance Q & A column at one of the leading English Newspapers of Saudi Arabia. He has reviewed and edited many books including joint material in association with CPCU (The Institutes, USA). He is also the author of books "Reinsurance for Beginners", "Customer Advice", "Savings on Motor Insurance", "Understanding Health Insurance" and "Pigeon and the cat plus other episodes".

He can be reached at mosakhan40@gmail.com. & www.generalawarenessforall.blogspot.com

www.ingramcontent.com/pod-product-compliance
Lightning Source LLC
Chambersburg PA
CBHW051907170526
45168CB00001B/273